G000020398

BIRDS

A GUIDE TO A MIXED COLLECTION

Published 1985 by Merehurst Press
5 Great James Street
London WC1N 3DA

© Copyright 1985 Merehurst Limited

ISBN 0 948075 00 7

Typeset by V & M Graphics Ltd, Aylesbury, Bucks
Printed in Spain by Printer Industria Grafica SA, Barcelona
Additional photographs supplied by Aquila Photographics
D.L.B. 41032-1984

ACKNOWLEDGEMENTS
I am deeply indebted to some fellow enthusiasts, without whose assistance this book
would not have been possible: Editor, Ken Denham, and eminent parrot authority,
Rosemary Low, who provided helpful guidance as well as technical expertise; Eric
Barlow, Michael Plose and Colin Waterman, who were kind enough to provide many of
their own photographs; Designer, Roger Daniels, who admits to a newly discovered
interest in bird-keeping; and all at Lansdowne-Rigby International, who have given me
the opportunity to realise a long cherished dream in the publication of this book.

Cage and Aviary Newspaper
A. C. Hughes
John McKenzie
Joe Mitchell
The Zoological Society of London
Drawings by Tony Garrett

A GUIDE TO A MIXED COLLECTION

IRENE CHRISTIE

CONSULTANT EDITOR: KEN DENHAM
FOREWORD BY ROSEMARY LOW

MEREHURST PRESS
LONDON

CONTENTS

FOREWORD by Rosemary Low   PAGE 5

INTRODUCTION   PAGE 6

PART 1

1 THE AVIARY   PAGE 7
Accommodation A description of outdoor and indoor aviaries, including details of design, location, protection from vermin and predators, heating, lighting and ideas on aviaries as a room feature.
Plants A selection of trees, shrubs and climbing plants suitable for the outdoor aviary, with descriptions of the conditions which suit them.
Equipment A list of equipment needed for bird care and aviary maintenance, including feeding and drinking utensils, perches, bird baths and pools, nest boxes and baskets, safety doors and first aid box.

2 FEEDING   PAGE 22
General dietary information, plus detailed feeding requirements of seedeating and softbill species.

3 BREEDING   PAGE 27
A description of the stages in breeding with notes on pairing birds, courtship and display, selection of nesting sites, how to aid the rearing of healthy chicks, foster parents, hand rearing and close and split ringing chicks.

4 AILMENTS   PAGE 35
An alphabetical guide to the most common ailments and simple methods of treatment, plus notes on first aid and hospital cages.

5 EXHIBITING AND PHOTOGRAPHING BIRDS   PAGE 41
Advice on successful exhibiting, with information on show cages, how to fill in entry forms and how to prepare birds for the show bench. Some helpful hints on camera equipment for photographing birds, colour and black and white photography, suggested types of birds to photograph and attractive locations.

PART 2

6 HOW TO SELECT COMPATIBLE BIRDS   PAGE 50
Advice on how to choose healthy specimens, how to treat newly purchased birds and how to select compatible birds for a mixed collection. Eight "compatibility groups" are described, each group made up of seedeaters and softbills, including parrotlike species, that live contentedly together without aggression. Each "compatibility group" is coded with a symbol for cross reference.

7 SUITABLE SPECIES FOR A MIXED COLLECTION   PAGE 54
An alphabetical list of 71 birds suitable for keeping in a mixed collection with notes on their origin, size, appearance, diet, habits and breeding potential. Each bird is coded with a symbol to identify the "compatibility group" to which it belongs for quick and easy identification.

8 UNUSUAL SPECIES FOR A MIXED COLLECTION   PAGE 127
A selection of 14 unusual birds which can only be kept with a small number of companions of certain types.

GLOSSARY   PAGE 140

INDEX   PAGE 142

Rosemary Low is an internationally recognised authority on the keeping of birds in captivity. She has travelled the world lecturing at symposiums, and is author of many books. I am indebted to her for her interest in this book, and for her advice and encouragement.

Having had the pleasure to work on the weekly magazine *Cage and Aviary Birds* for 15 years, daily answering questions posed by beginners, I am well aware of how basic is the advice they seek. BIRDS – A GUIDE TO A MIXED COLLECTION, written with the less experienced keeper in mind, answers those points which are a matter of mystery to the beginner. Which birds can I keep together? Are they hardy? Can I expect them to breed? Which plants are suitable for my aviary?

Details which seem obvious to the breeder of a few years' standing are given within these pages, together with much valuable advice on all aspects of maintenance of the birds and their accommodation. This is a useful introduction to the beginner who is advised not to start too ambitiously. If he or she builds up a collection gradually, commencing with the hardier and less expensive species, disappointments will be fewer and enjoyment greater.

Aviculture is one of the most enjoyable and relaxing pastimes in which it is possible to indulge. It can develop into more than that – a means of conserving some of the threatened birds of the world. The captive populations of certain species, whose natural habitat has been largely or even totally destroyed, is greater than the wild populations, and it is private aviculturists, as much as zoos, who have been responsible for this development. It is now accepted that aviculture has become a major conservation tool as well as a rewarding hobby which can be enjoyed at all levels.

Rosemary Low

ROSEMARY LOW.

INTRODUCTION

The aim of this book is to assist and encourage anyone who wishes to maintain a mixed collection of birds, with practical advice for both novice and experienced bird keeper.

If kept with unsuitable companions, birds can be aggressive and unhappy. This easy to follow guide enables the fancier to select species that live together contentedly, and a simple system of coding allows each of the 71 birds described in detail in Chapter 7 to be grouped into eight selections of compatible birds. There is also a chapter at the end of the book on some unusual species of birds and their requirements to interest the more experienced fancier, who wishes to enlarge the scope of his hobby.

There is detailed advice on planning an indoor and outdoor aviary, with notes on equipment, suitable plants, feeding, breeding, ailments exhibiting and photographing birds. I wish you every success and many hours of enjoyable bird keeping.

IRENE CHRISTIE

THE AVIARY

ACCOMMODATION

AN AVIARY REQUIRES careful planning before birds are introduced to their new quarters. Accommodation is the first consideration. While a single bird can be housed successfully in a cage, larger numbers require more thought and planning and far more space. Bird keeping may start on a very small scale, but this should not mean that it is undertaken in a haphazard manner. Sensible precautions must be taken from the outset.

All types of bird live healthily and contentedly in captivity for much longer if they can exercise their wings frequently. Being able to exercise prevents birds from becoming overweight and sluggish. In the wild, birds forage actively for their food, but captive birds have no such need. Their diet, rich in all the necessary ingredients, is readily available, provided by a thoughtful owner who may not at first realise that this can create problems. Aviaries offer better conditions for birds than cages, as the aviary allows plenty of exercise. If keeping pairs of birds for breeding, it is essential to allow the maximum amount of space for flying, nesting, roosting and feeding. Sooner or later most serious fanciers opt for either an outdoor or indoor aviary to house their growing bird collection. Most start out with the odd pair of birds, or even just one, but bird keeping has a tendency to develop far beyond the original intention.

It must be stressed that keeping pairs of birds in mixed collections may lead to squabbles, particularly at the time of year when pairs come into breeding condition. For this reason, it is important to select birds carefully. Turn to Chapters 6 and 7 for advice on how to choose compatible species. No such problem occurs if only cock (male) birds of different species are kept together. Indeed many fanciers do just this, choosing them for their colourful plumage or singing ability. However, much depends on the individual nature of the birds concerned, as those of a placid nature mingle well even in small quarters. It is a wise practice, however, to allow as much space as possible when keeping mixed pairs together.

THE OUTDOOR AVIARY

Outdoor accommodation for birds consists of a shelter or bird room for roosting and a flight for exercise. It should be planned so as to allow easy entrance for the owner with minimum disturbance and so that the birds can be locked in at night or during bad weather. The spot chosen should offer the maximum in light and fresh air, with protection from wet, cold or windy weather and also from excessive heat.

The shelter is the most important part of the aviary and needs to be designed with care to ensure that the owner can feed and

An outdoor aviary with shelter

maintain birds with minimum effort. The shelter must be damp- and draught-proof, yet with sufficient ventilation to give the birds ample supplies of fresh air during hot summer weather. A shelter built above ground level gives the greatest protection from vermin and damp.

The flight is constructed from wire mesh netting. The mesh must be small enough to prevent the birds from escaping and mice and other vermin from entering. A very small size mesh is needed for finches.

When using glass in the flight or shelter, it is most important to cover the inside with mesh netting for birds can easily fly into glass and injure or kill themselves.

When planning aviaries, whether outdoor or indoor, there are several points to bear in mind. Height in an aviary is important since most birds like to fly up, and usually favour the highest possible position for roosting. To encourage the birds to roost under cover, the highest roosting point should be located inside the shelter. Also take into account that at times it is necessary to catch birds with a net. An extra high aviary may be needed if very large species are to be kept. The larger the aviary, the greater the cost of materials for its construction.

The space available often dictates the size of aviary. Some bird fanciers start by fencing in large areas of garden complete with trees, shrubs, lawn or pool, and many devote increasing areas of their garden as time and further birds make it necessary. A large aviary allows the enthusiast to add to the collection without overcrowding and without having to re-plan or alter the original accommodation.

Length is the next most significant consideration when planning the aviary. As great a length as possible should be allowed. Width is not as important, but from the point of view of appearance, the proportions should be well balanced.

Drainage in the flight is very important. If soil has good natural drainage, a normal earth floor topped up with fine grade gravel and perhaps a little freshly washed river sand is sufficient. Alternatively, turf may be laid, which should be allowed to settle well before birds are introduced to the aviary.

The floor of the aviary flight should be either concrete or paving stones for maximum ease of cleaning, or else natural earth or grass. If the aviary is not being planted out, plants in pots or tubs may be

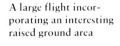
A large flight incorporating an interesting raised ground area

substituted to provide foliage. The floor of the shelter should be concrete or, for more warmth, concrete lined with timber.

Concrete flooring may be more expensive, but it is easy to keep clean and maintain. Even if a soil floor is preferred, the walls surrounding the flight and shelter should be of cement with the foundations taken to a depth of at least 46 cm (18 in). The walls should slope away from the base to give good drainage. This also prevents mice, rats and other vermin from digging their way in. Concrete flooring should be sloped to give drainage and protection in the same way. It may be hosed for ease of cleaning. Concrete floors may be covered with a layer of sand. Occasionally, fanciers use wood shavings but the dust from these can cause eye infections in birds. Sand and peat moss are useful floor coverings to protect birds from damp and to absorb their droppings. Earth floors should be forked over at least once a year and the top dressed with lime and fresh sand.

In countries with a hot climate, where earth floors are practical, the dry weather provides birds with an opportunity to dust bathe when the soil becomes dry and powdery. A dry floor is an important requirement for birds since chilling can be very harmful. Species, such as quail, which spend a lot of time on the ground, are the most susceptible.

It is advisable to try to prevent cats from walking over the roof of the aviary and frightening the birds. Try to suspend plastic mesh netting, stretched fairly tight, about 23 cm (9 in) above the roof. It is then impossible for cats to maintain a foothold. This is kinder than using barbed wire or broken glass which may cause injury to animals.

The most dangerous predators are usually rodents. Careful precautions must be taken and a concrete floored aviary is fairly easy to protect. For peace of mind, take the depth of concrete under the aviary and shelter floor to as much as 76 cm (30 in), making it very difficult for rats and larger predators to gain entry. Woodwork is vulnerable to rodents: once they start trying to gnaw their way in, they often return to complete the job, night after night. If the aviary has an earth floor, wire netting borders should be sunk to a depth of at least 61 cm (24 in) below the ground. The trench must be deep and wide

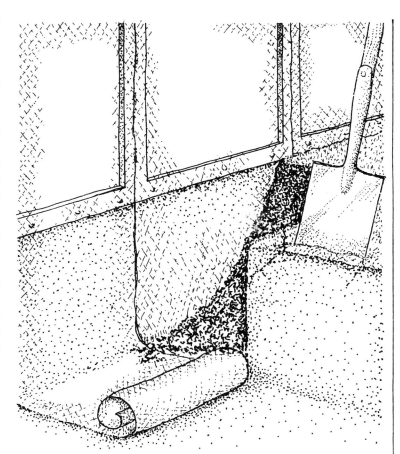

enough to enable the wire netting to be bent outwards. Broken glass can be buried in the trench on the outside of the wire to discourage burrowing.

While mice are not quite as dangerous, they are undesirable. They are also able to get through mesh even of a very small diameter. They often frighten birds who may fly into shelter walls or flight wire and injure or kill themselves. If birds are sitting, they may be frightened off their nests and desert their young. If mice get into nests, they can injure the young unfledged birds, tumble them out of the nest or eat them. Mice droppings may contaminate bird food, which can be very serious. To stop mice from entering the flight or shelter, surround the base area with glass or sheet metal at least 30 cm (12 in) to 51 cm (20 in) in depth. Food dishes in the aviary should be sited above ground level to avoid mice droppings or other contamination. This is not possible when keeping ground birds, such as species of quail.

Aviaries should be built with a low door or safety porch to prevent birds escaping when their owner enters or leaves the

How to sink a wire netting border to keep out mice and other vermin

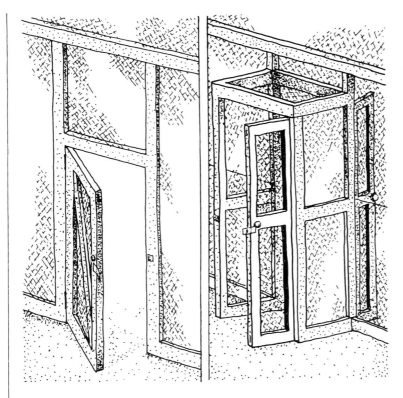

Left: a low door and
Right: a door with
safety porch, both
suitable for an aviary
entrance as they prevent
birds escaping

accommodation. Doors may be fitted with springs to ensure speedy, efficient closure.

Electric lighting inside the shelter and outside in the flight is indispensable. It enables the owner to check the birds on dark evenings, lock them away for the night, do any necessary chores and make sure there are no prowling cats or other predators in the vicinity. Automatic time-controlled dimmer switches are recommended, because birds dislike a change from light to sudden darkness and often panic and injure themselves, if the light is not reduced gradually. To prevent birds from burning themselves surround each bulb with a wire mesh screen several inches away from its surface.

Birds only feed in the light. In some areas, it is advisable to switch on the lights for extra hours in winter, particularly in the morning, to give more feeding time to ensure good health. This is particularly important if birds are breeding in winter as they must be able to feed their chicks in the light. Many birds insist on going to nest at unsuitable times, so this is an important consideration.

The next question is that of warmth. If the shelter is well insulated from damp and draughts, this is a very good start. In exposed areas, the flight may be protected from harsh winds by placing boards on one or more of its sides. Part of the roof may also be covered by placing green plasti-glass or similar material at a sloping angle to allow rain to run off easily. Many birds enjoy sitting in fine rain, which is good for their plumage. Most try to retreat from a heavy downpour, which is not good for them.

In cold areas, the maximum temperature recommended for bird shelters or rooms is 15°C (60°F), since a higher temperature is not only costly to maintain, but is likely to weaken the birds. Only a hospital cage should be maintained at a higher temperature, which must be reduced gradually as the bird recovers. Radiators, hot water pipes and thermostatically controlled tubular heaters or fans may be used in the shelter. Some fanciers use oil or calor gas heaters, but these are not recommended since, if not properly maintained, they give off fumes which can make birds ill. There is also a risk of fire. Some birds winter successfully in a shelter that is dry and damp-proof without any extra heat, but others benefit from a little help as the nights turn frosty. A light bulb may often be sufficient. If in doubt, it is better to keep the birds a little warmer than necessary, as heat may be gradually reduced later. This is easier than treating a bird with pneumonia.

Many birds enjoy basking in sunshine in the morning light, so, if possible, the flight should be positioned to catch the morning sun rays. In warm climates, the afternoon sun may be too hot, so care should be taken to provide plenty of facilities offering shade and cool, such as bushes, trees, water fountains, sprays and small pools. Pools must be shallow, so that young or small birds do not drown.

Humidity should be provided in the bird shelter to prevent the plumage drying out and becoming brittle. It is also important to have plenty of fresh air circulating. A small portable humidifier running on electricity may be used or try placing a pan of boiling water in the shelter each day. Do make sure that the saucepan is covered with a net just in case an unwary bird attempts to dive in. A constant circulation of fresh air may be maintained by a low inlet, which should be proofed against mice, and an air outlet on the opposite wall of the shelter, high up under the eaves.

These should be located away from perching birds, so that they are not caught in a draught.

In summer, the windows of the shelter or bird house may be left open and covered with wire netting. Do not leave them open at night without making sure that the shelter is protected from invaders. All glass must be covered with wire netting.

The shelter should be as light as possible to encourage birds to enter. The entry hole, or "bobhole" as it is often called, should be located in a high position. A further larger door may surround the bobhole to be opened in fine weather or at other times for the owner's convenience. A sliding bobhole is often a good idea for shutting the birds in at night with ease.

Wire netting comes in a variety of sizes and weights and the mesh chosen varies according to the types of birds to be housed. Fanciers often paint the netting with black, lead-free enamel, making the birds easier to view. Welded wire mesh is more expensive than ordinary aviary wire netting, but is neater when finished and also easier to work on. It lasts longer, and is worth the initial extra outlay.

Ready-made aviaries of many different shapes and sizes may be purchased complete or in sectional panels from specialist suppliers. However, a home-designed and built structure is likely to be a more individual model, tailor-made to requirements. First, measure the area available and decide how large the flight and shelter are to be. Using some graph paper, draw up a scale plan of the ground area and then draw both front and rear views of the accommodation to scale. Simple drawings are sufficient to check all measurements.

A lean-to aviary against a garden or house wall comprising flight and shelter, is one of the most popular styles. A strong, sloping roof may be constructed from timber which should be given a weather-proof coating. The roof may be entirely of

A spacious flight with timber-clad shelter showing the main requirements. Note the glass window in the shelter for light, the sliding door to the bob-hole to allow birds to be shut into the shelter without entering the aviary and the lower door for ease of cleaning the shelter. For protection against vermin, the floor of the aviary is above ground level.

Top: a simple lean-to
aviary with sloping roof
allowing quick drainage

Above: a large, open
flight fixed to a
convenient wall

timber or may be half netting and half
timber.

Circular and octagonal aviaries are
often popular since they give a good all-
round view of the birds, but generally
rectangular or square structures utilise
available space far more effectively and
economically. All timbers used in aviary
construction should be treated with
creosote to prevent mites and other
infestation. This treatment also prevents
wood from rotting due to damp and once
dry creosote does not affect the occupants.

There are many alarm systems that can
be purchased to help ensure the security of
an outdoor aviary and to help protect
valuable birds against theft.

THE INDOOR AVIARY

Some fanciers prefer to house their birds
indoors. This may be for a variety of
reasons: some like to have their collection
nearby to enjoy watching the birds,
especially those people confined to their

home due to ill-health or old age. If valuable birds are kept, an indoor aviary provides better security. The birds are totally secure from predators, inclement weather, night frights and thieves. This is worth bearing in mind, since birds command such high prices that theft is on the increase.

Careful planning is needed for the indoor aviary to make sure it is suitable for birds, easy to clean and maintain. Depending on the type of birds to be kept, there are many different forms of indoor flight which the prospective fancier can purchase or construct himself.

Small softbills may be housed in a flight with a glass front, perhaps built into an alcove or chimney breast. Seedeaters too, can be housed in such a setting, creating an interesting focal point in a room. If a complete spare room is available, it is a simple matter to construct a floor-to-ceiling wire mesh flight and of course it is not necessary to include a shelter. The base may be made of wood in the form of a tray and covered with a material which is easy to clean and lined with newspaper, frequently changed. To prevent seed husks from travelling outside the flight area, fix plastic sheeting across the lower half of the flight.

When keeping birds indoors, give their quarters a weekly spray with a good quality anti-mite preparation, paying particular attention to ends of perches and woodwork of any kind. Mites can be more troublesome indoors than in an outside aviary. Try to encourage the presence of spiders since they destroy red mites. There should be no problems with mice and other vermin. In warm summer weather, strict cleanliness must be observed with regard to food and droppings, particularly if keeping softbills, since flies are encouraged if hygiene is neglected.

Keeping birds indoors creates more chores about the house. The birds need regular spraying with a hand spray containing warm water or else a bird bath in order to maintain good plumage. This aspect of their care must not be neglected, or feathers become dry and brittle. Preening is an activity which is undertaken by birds as part of their daily routine to distribute oil from their oil gland through their feathers. Without regular preening, feathers soon lose their lustre and sheen. A good spray or

Above: an indoor aviary built into an alcove. Note the side door for ease of access, top light and glass surround to prevent seed from being thrown out by the birds

Left: a cage fixed above a cupboard and used as an indoor aviary and room divider

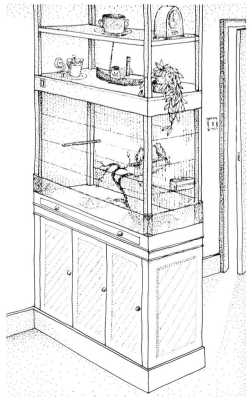

13

Far right: a Victoria
Crowned Pigeon
enjoying a dust bath

Right: an indoor aviary
on a window ledge
which allows the
window to be opened in
suitable weather

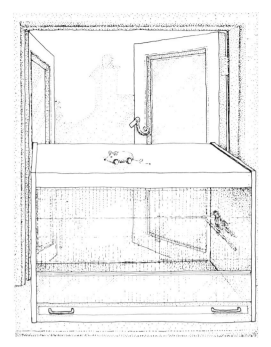

bath always encourages a bird to preen
actively. Some birds enjoy a dust bath and
a tray may be filled with a mixture of fine
soil and sand for this purpose.

A conservatory makes ideal housing for
an indoor mixed collection, but any spare
room can be made into a bird haven by
adding plants and perhaps even a small
indoor fountain.

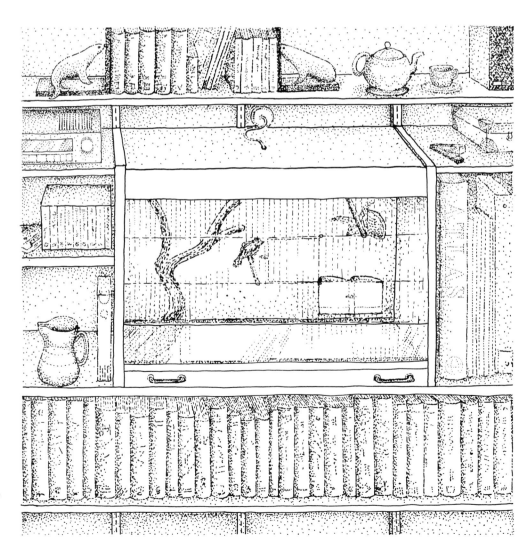

Right: an interesting
indoor aviary built into
a bookcase. Note the
top flap for the
overhead light

PLANTS

Once the aviary has been built the next step is to choose plants to enhance even the most simple aviary. These may be planted out or placed in troughs, planters and tubs in selected areas.

Many species are encouraged to breed by the shelter and seclusion of a densely planted aviary. Plants also attract insects, which the birds are able to catch and eat.

Climbing plants, such as vines and roses, are useful as a covering for aviary netting, giving shade and a pleasing appearance. However, beware of any plants with thorns or spikes which may create difficulties when catching birds.

It is a good idea to install plants before introducing birds to the aviary. If possible, allow some time for plants to become established before introducing stock.

Some birds, particularly the parrotlike species, may damage plants with their beaks. Laurel and rhododendron are both poisonous to budgerigars and parrakeets and so must never be included. It may be necessary to clean some of the plants occasionally if they are soiled with droppings, though generally normal rainfall will wash away any mess.

The following is a list of trees and plants which are safe to include in an aviary.

BERBERIS (*Mahonia aquifolium*)
An evergreen shrub which grows quickly and spreads well. It bears yellow flowers which fruit into blackish-blue, satin-like berries. The leaves turn dark, almost purple in winter months. Another variety of Berberis (*Mahonia hortorum*) is very similar with the same berries but grows to a greater height.

BLACKBERRY (*Rubus fructicosus*)
A hardy species which does well in any type of soil, but prefers damp, shady conditions. It is a fast-growing bush which spreads very well. Birds love the luscious dark fruit and many insects are also attracted by it.

A well planned, attractive, outdoor aviary which should encourage birds to breed

BOX (*Buxus sempervirens*)
A useful hedging shrub, preferred by small waxbills for nesting. It may be trimmed neatly for nesting birds during the breeding season but left to grow freely for shelter at other times. A very practical evergreen which flourishes in all soils in sun or shade.

CONIFER
There are numerous types of conifers suitable for aviaries. They have a pleasing appearance and tough foliage which withstands the attentions of sharp beaks. Dwarf conifers come in many different shapes and sizes and leaf colour. Many are, in fact, quite large and grow rapidly. From the great variety available, two recommended ones are:

NANA (*Picea mariana*) Dwarf Conifer
A slow-growing, compact, round-shaped spruce with blue-grey foliage. Birds, especially small finches, love climbing about in this. As most of the conifer family, it prefers sandy soil and is very hardy.

LITTLE GEM (*Picea abies*) Dwarf Conifer
This grows in an attractive, dense, round green ball and attracts red spider mites, which are enjoyed by many birds. It grows well in sandy soil.

COTONEASTER (*Cotoneaster horizontalis* and *Rotundifolia*)
The *Cotoneaster horizontalis* is a lovely spreading plant which looks very attractive with its pinky-white flowers. The *Cotoneaster Rotundifolia* grows upright and has larger blossoms. Both types produce red berries and require a sunny area which is not too wet. The foliage lasts all the year round.

ENGLISH HOLLY (*Ilex aquifolium*) or **AMERICAN HOLLY** (*Ilex opeca*)
Holly requires a sunny area but soil that is not too dry. Male and female bushes should be obtained if possible and planted side by side to ensure a mass of lovely bright red berries. Holly may be used for hedging, particularly the *Pyramidalis* variety, which provides useful nesting sites. This species also produces plenty of fruit.

ENGLISH IVY (*Hedera helix*)
A very useful, attractive climber suitable for covering aviary netting or walls. Too much sun makes this plant shrivel, preferring a shady spot. The evergreen colour is maintained throughout the year. The tiny flowers produce black berries which are occasionally eaten by birds. There is a larger-leaved variety called Hibernica which is also attractive.

EUROPEAN ELDERBERRY (*Sambucus nigra*) or **COMMON ELDERBERRY** (*Sambucus Canadensis*) or **RED ELDERBERRY** (*Sambucus pubens*)
Grows rapidly in most types of soil with

An indoor, planted flight with a brick surround

sufficient humus. It needs plenty of sun and moisture to produce lush groups of berries eagerly devoured by birds. The berries also attract insects to tempt the insect-eating species. It is easy to grow and maintain.

FORSYTHIA (*Forsythia spectabilis*)

The tough woody stems are impervious to beaks, and the profusion of yellow flowers makes a beautiful sight. It provides good shade, cover and useful nesting sites.

HAWTHORN (*Crataegus monogyna*)

A fairly tall tree which is very suitable for nesting purposes. It bears pleasantly scented, pinky-red flowers which produce bright red berries. These are enjoyed by many species of birds. Hawthorn does well in most soils in a sunny area.

HONEYSUCKLE (*Lonicera*)

A versatile climbing plant which looks very attractive and provides useful nesting sites. The lush flowers smell delicious and attract insects well.

JUNIPER

Junipers are recommended and there are a great number from which to choose. One of the most attractive is:

BLUE STAR (*Juniperus squamata*)

An adaptable and hardy Juniper, the steel blue foliage is attractive. It grows very quickly and occasionally needs to be trimmed. In three years, this Juniper can grow to four times its original size.

MOCK ORANGE BLOSSOM (*Philadelphus coronarius*)

This delightfully scented shrub can grow very tall. A good choice as the blooms attract plenty of insects. It is a very hardy plant.

RASPBERRY (*Rubus*)

This needs similar conditions to the Blackberry. The rich, red fruit is also loved by birds.

RUSSIAN VINE (*Polygonu...*)

Another very popular, rampant climbing

plant suitable for aviaries. It rapidly covers aviary netting.

SNOWBERRY (*Symphoricarpus abus*)
A hardy, bushy shrub which bears a profusion of pink blossom and fruits into white berries, which are much appreciated by the small species of quail.

WEEPING WILLOW (*Salix babylonica*)
If plenty of space is available and waterfowl are kept on a small pond or lake, then reeds, rushes and this willow are very attractive.

WILD ROSE (*Rose multiflora*)
There are many different varieties of wild rose. All make excellent and picturesque climbing plants for aviaries. They may also be used as nesting sites and they invite large numbers of useful insects. Sunny areas and damp soil are favoured.

An aviary roof showing a lush covering of fast-growing Russian Vine

EQUIPMENT

Once the aviary is constructed and plants installed, equipment must be considered. Birds need perches, drinkers, feeding dishes, nest boxes and baskets. The owner needs some tools for aviary maintenance and cleaning.

PERCHES

These should vary in thickness to exercise the birds' feet properly. Dowel perching may be bought in pet stores and cut into various lengths as required. Natural perching should also be provided in the form of branches of different sizes. It is recommended that both natural and dowel perching are provided, perhaps dowel in the shelter and natural in the flight. Incorrect perches often cause birds toenails to grow too long and curve into uncomfortable shapes. Metal perches should never be used. Some of the perches should be sited quite high up, particularly in the shelter for roosting. These should be the thinnest perches, which birds usually prefer.

Softbilled birds wipe their beaks on perches constantly, so natural perches should be replaced frequently, while dowel perches are easy to wash. Birds also foul their perches with their droppings. Careful positioning of perches helps to prevent this, but dirty perches must always be replaced or washed. Many birds enjoy stripping the bark from branches and for this purpose, apple wood is a very good choice.

Above: a useful seed-saving hopper

FEEDING DISHES AND DRINKERS

Feeding dishes should be placed where they are not fouled by bird droppings. Different containers are required for various types of birds. Seedeaters need a dish which is fairly deep for mixed millets and plain canary seed. If several different dishes for millets and a separate one for canary seed are provided, it is possible to identify the birds preference and balance their diet. Further containers should hold min-

Left: a planted aviary housing Diamond Sparrows and Zebra Finches

eral grit, canary song food and insectile mixtures, dietary supplements and any other favoured snacks, such as apple, which some seedeaters really enjoy.

Food and water dishes may be made of china, earthenware, glass or plastic and should be scalded before use. Metal containers are often used for parrotlike species. Dietary supplements should not be given in metal containers because a chemical reaction may take place. Automatic bird seed feeders, which are efficient and reliable, may be purchased at pet stores.

Clear plastic or glass drinkers of tubular design keep water fresh and clean, although some birds tend to use them as shower baths. These are essential for nectar feeding softbills. Any algae forming on the inside must be removed by regular, thorough cleaning. Some very fancy feeding and drinking equipment can be purchased from pet stores, so it is up to the individual how much money to spend. Simple, inexpensive dishes are usually quite adequate. Ease of cleaning is always a point to remember when making a decision.

Several feeding positions in an aviary prevent any squabbling or bullying over meals and give all the birds a fair chance at feeding time.

It is always better to place food above ground level, except for quail and other similar ground dwellers. Wild bird feeders on stands are a useful buy for aviaries, since they keep food in a clean condition well above the ground.

Above: a waterfall makes an attractive and useful feature in an aviary

Below: an easily constructed wooden case suitable for carrying drinking tubes

BIRD BATHS AND POOLS
The type of bird bath normally purchased for a garden can look very attractive within an aviary. Some ornamental stone baths look particularly elegant. Water pumps may be used to provide a fountain which can be another pleasing feature, but it may take some birds a little time to become accustomed to it. Bird baths and pools should always be shallow to avoid young birds drowning. The type of plastic pool normally used for small fish can be used if stones are placed on the bottom of the pool to reduce the depth. This again can accommodate a fountain or even a waterfall. Baths and pools should have clean, clear water at all times and never be allowed to stagnate. If possible, provide fresh running water.

ORNAMENTS

Some fanciers choose to incorporate ornaments in their aviaries. There are some attractive stone statues of animals, birds and other figures which can be bought in garden centres to add further interest to the aviary.

NESTING BOXES AND BASKETS

Nest boxes for finches, with a round entrance or a half square front, should be positioned at varying heights in the aviary. Cover should be given in the form of bundles of reeds, branches, heather or hedging screens. Tree bark may also be used for this purpose, and shrubs also provide good cover. Wicker nest baskets are very popular and come in various globular shapes with entrance holes in different positions, but need to be sprayed regularly with mild disinfectant as they attract mites and other tiny insects. A mild disinfectant will not harm the birds.

Some species favour canary nest pans or nest logs. The greater the variety of nest sites offered, the better the chance of birds attempting to breed. Canaries nest happily in the standard canary nest pan and budgerigars in the normal size standard budgerigar nesting boxes. Coconut shells may be wired together to make an unusual nesting site for small finches. Care must be taken to ensure there is nothing for the birds to catch their feet on. Bundles of hay and dried grasses may be packed into mesh bags and hung up for the use of nesting birds.

Parrakeets and cockatiels need larger nest boxes and logs than smaller birds, although cockatiels use a budgerigar nest box quite frequently. It is often surprising

An ornamental stone owl looks attractive in an outdoor aviary

how small a box some birds select if they are keen to breed, as perhaps a small box creates a feeling of security. It is interesting to watch birds choose a nest site and often the most unlikely spot is the final choice.

WIRED-IN SAFETY DOOR

A wired-in safety door is essential to prevent birds escaping. This should also allow the owner to feed the birds without entering the aviary, thus creating a minimum of disturbance.

OTHER SUNDRY EQUIPMENT
RACKS for green food
CLIPS for hanging up cuttle fish bone
BINS for seed storage
CATCHING NET
BROOM
CLEANING UTENSILS including a
    scraper for removal of droppings
TRAVEL CAGE
BIRD BATH CAGE
HAND MIST SPRAY

FIRST AID BOX: This should contain such items as Hydrogen Peroxide to stop bleeding, cotton wool, disinfectant and nail clippers. A torch is another useful item.
HOSPITAL CAGE: Used to provide sick birds with controlled heat. This can be a simple box cage with a light bulb fitted inside. Ensure it has adequate ventilation.
INCUBATOR: Used for hatching eggs. There are many excellent makes available from specialist suppliers.

CHAPTER 2

FEEDING

CORRECT NUTRITION is one of the most important factors for healthy and contented birds. In the case of seedeaters, the seed diet is straightforward. The softbill fancier must take extra care, since the requirements of the many species of softbill are more exacting than those of seedeaters.

It is always worthwhile making that little extra effort to provide as wide a variety of food as possible. Additional nutrition and favoured tit-bits make the difference between the average healthy bird and the specimen with excellent show potential that is also eager to breed.

Cleanliness and hygiene are also of great importance. Those intending to keep waterfowl should always be careful to see that their food does not become messy and contaminated and is located well away from their pond or lake.

In general, hot weather causes the most problems with regard to following hygienic feeding routines. With nectar feeding softbills however, cold weather is a nuisance, if severe enough to freeze the nectar mixture in its plastic tubes.

In common with humans, all birds require the following vitamins:

Vitamin A Promotes healthy skin and feathers and is essential for young birds.
Vitamin B Needed for the central nervous system, energy and vitality.
Vitamin C Prevents skin disease.
Vitamin D Aids formation of bones.
Vitamin E Prevents sterility and aids fertility.

DIET FOR SEEDEATING BIRDS

Dry bird seed normally provides a satisfactory diet, but many experienced fanciers maintain that a diet of soaked and sprouted seed proves more nutritious. Cheap seed should be avoided since it usually contains a great deal of dust and proves difficult to germinate. The value of soaked and sprouted seed cannot be stressed too strongly. Birds with young must be provided with ample quantities of good quality soaked and sprouted seeds to successfully rear healthy broods. The vitamin content of sprouted seed is extremely high. Seeds should be soaked in cold water for 24 hours, then washed, drained and left to sprout in a warm place, until the shoots are about 6 mm ($\frac{1}{4}$ in) long. This can take two to four days, according to the temperature.

The most universally popular seeds are the four varieties of millet seed: white, panicum, Japanese and red millet. These are usually mixed together. Plain canary seed is the next most frequently used with other seeds fed as required. Maw seed, rape, linseed and hemp seed (if available) and the black niger seed are useful, particularly during cold weather when body fat needs to be maintained. Hulled oats, groats and sunflower seed are usually fed to larger species. Parrotlike birds need adequate supplies of sunflower seeds and many eat maize and peanuts too.

A simple extra is clear honey which may be mixed with water in drinkers or even with seed for birds with young in the nest. Raw egg yolk may also be mixed with seed. Stale bread, which has been well soaked, should be crumbled into small pieces and may have a little milk poured over it to form an ideal rearing aid. Wholemeal bread is even better than white bread. Any leftovers must be removed quickly, especially in warm weather, lest the milk turn sour. Alternatively, the bread can be soaked in water, which is better if the remains cannot be removed promptly. Never use fresh bread for this purpose; it is heavy even on human digestion, but can prove fatal to young birds.

Ample supplies of grit and cuttle fish bone are essential. Grit comes in several forms including oystershell, crushed granite and slate. Proprietary tonic grit in packet form may be purchased at pet food stores. It contains several vital minerals including salt, iron oxide, calcium, lime, phosphorus and a little charcoal. This preparation helps birds to masticate seed in the crop and therefore to digest their food properly. The calcium in cuttlefish bone is very high. Cuttlefish bone may be given both whole flaked into small thin slivers. Birds enjoy nibbling the bone, which helps to keep their beaks in good condition.

Chicken egg shells are a very worthwhile source of added calcium, particularly important to hens during the breeding season to help form their own healthy egg shells. Clean egg shells should be baked in the oven until very brittle and crushed into fine particles before feeding.

Charcoal is relished by certain seedeaters, especially Australian finches. All types of grit should be provided in a separate dish to discourage birds from taking only their favourite kind from a selection.

If practical, birds are much easier to feed and manage when annual or perennial seeding grasses are grown in the aviary. With these semi-ripe seeds available many types of birds successfully rear broods with little more than a hard seed diet.

Fresh greenfood should be fed on a regular basis as sporadic feeding can cause stomach upsets. New stock should be introduced to greenfood gradually and quantities increased as they become accustomed to it. Take care that any greenstuff has been obtained from areas free from insecticide spray, and that the food is always washed carefully. Chickweed (*Stellaria media*) is an important source of Vitamin E. Lettuce, dandelion and spinach are all useful. Among suitable seeding weeds are plantain (*Plantago lanceolata*), groundsel (*Senecio vulgaris*), shepherd's purse (*Capsella bursa pastoris*) and clover (*Trifolium pratense*). Thistles, such as *Carduus* and *Cirsium*, are enjoyed by many birds including the goldfinch. Frozen greenfood should never be given, as it chills the stomach. Some birds use left-over greenstuff in their nests during the breeding season and this damp material often helps in softening the egg shells, allowing the chicks to hatch easily.

Cod liver oil is a highly beneficial addition to the seed during cold weather and particularly in the breeding season to help prevent egg binding in young hens. Add 5 ml (1 teaspoon) of stabilised cod liver oil to ½ kg (2 lb 3 oz) of mixed millet, shake well and allow to stand for 24 hours before feeding to birds. Any uneaten oiled seed should be removed after a further 24 hours to prevent it from becoming rancid. This seed can then be washed and allowed to sprout before feeding to the birds so that it is not wasted. Oiled seed should be fed about once a month during summer and weekly in winter.

A liquid multi-vitamin preparation may be added to the birds' drinkers, if desired. Two drops are sufficient added to water in a standard 50 cc (1 pint) drinker every other day.

During the breeding season, breeding pairs may be supplied with proprietary brand canary rearing food mixed with finely mashed hard boiled egg. This is a nourishing food for regurgitation by the parents for feeding to their young. It is best to start the parents on this before the young arrive, so they become accustomed to the mixture, and to check that they are feeding well. It should be given in the morning and uneaten mixture thrown away by dusk, or earlier in very warm regions, to ensure it is not tainted.

Ground birds, such as quail and small doves, require a seed mixture comprising equal parts of canary seed, mixed millets and a small quantity of hemp (if available) and groats. Wheat should be added to the diet of larger quail. Since quail are avid consumers of insectivorous food, meal worms, beetles and fresh ants' eggs should be offered.

For parrotlike species, add sunflower seed, fresh peanuts, groats and a small amount of hemp (if available) to mixed millets and plain canary seed. Sunflower and peanuts should make up about half of the mixture. The greater the variety, the better.

Large parrakeets also enjoy other seeds such as buckwheat, whole oats, barley, wheat and maize. They enjoy small sweet apples, grapes, pears and bananas. All should be unbruised fruit of sound quality. They also like raw carrot and fresh sweetcorn (maize). They may also be given twigs to chew and they enjoy stripping the

Striped sunflower seed is a main item in the diet of parrotlike birds. It should be plump and hard.

bark off these. Many types of wood are suitable, except laurel and laburnum, which are poisonous and must never be used. Boiled sweetcorn (maize), should be fed in a separate dish, or its moisture makes seed turn mouldy.

Some birds prefer fruit containing seeds or pips and waste the flesh to reach them. Pomegranates are often enjoyed. Sponge cake soaked in a honey mixture may also be offered.

Parrotlike birds often suffer from a deficiency of Vitamin A in seed diets, so it is wise to provide a nectar mixture to rectify this. Two teaspoons of honey and two of rose hip syrup should be dissolved in water. If desired, add a few drops of a multi-vitamin preparation and perhaps alternate this with a meat extract on occasion for variety. This should become part of their regular diet and provides ample quantities of Vitamins A and D. Other alternatives, such as malt, condensed milk and honey, may also be offered mixed with water. This should be given in dishes rather than tubes for these species.

Most parrotlike birds love picking over a clod of earth with roots and grass attached. The trace elements manganese, iron, copper and zinc are often lacking in their diet and are provided in this way.

It is recommended that cooled boiled water is always given to small seedeaters, particularly Australian species, such as gouldians, who always seem to thrive better on this. It is difficult to prevent birds drinking from other sources when they are kept outside, but at least the water in their drinkers should be boiled.

A final point with regard to the feeding of seedeaters: Australia and the State of California in the U.S.A. declared the sale of hemp seed illegal some time ago. It is worth mentioning here that sunflower seed provides the same nutrients as hemp.

DIET FOR SOFTBILLED BIRDS

The most important point to remember when feeding softbills is that careful attention should be paid to hygiene. Most of the food that comprises their daily menu is perishable and should be freshly prepared at all times and any left-overs removed before they become tainted. Uneaten food left lying on the aviary floor must also be cleared away.

All softbills, including omnivorous, frugivorous, nectivorous, insectivorous or carnivorous types, require more complicated feeding routines than seedeaters. The diet for softbilled birds normally includes the following items.

Proprietary brands of both fine grade and coarse grade insectile mixtures for softbills can be obtained at pet food stores. Mixtures can also be made at home, but this is a task for the expert. The mixture should form a basic part of the diet, fine grade for the smaller species, including small insectivorous, omnivorous and frugivorous birds, and coarse grade for larger softbills, such as fruitsuckers, jays and starlings. Insectile mixtures are not perishable, but should be stored in airtight containers to preserve their moisture. These mixtures contain a well balanced blend of proteins, carbohydrates, vitamins and minerals.

Nectar mixture is important to all types of softbills and essential for the nectivorous species and should always be available. Proprietary brands of nectar powder may be purchased to be diluted with sugar and warm water as per the instructions on the individual packet. These mixtures are easy to prepare in the correct strength. They may be mixed with pure clear honey and warm water, instead of sugar, if desired. Honey contains less carbohydrate than sugar, so provides less energy but is not so fattening. A very active bird needs sugar, while a more lethargic species lives well on honey.

As many different types of fruit as possible should be offered to provide variety. It must be ripe, but not over ripe, and unbruised. Chop all fruit into small cubes. Oranges however may sometimes be cut in half and suspended by pieces of string near a favourite perching spot. Food should never be placed where the birds may foul it with their droppings.

Dried fruit, such as sultanas, currants and raisins, are rich in food value. They should be soaked for a few hours before feeding, and can be rather fattening, so should be fed in moderation. Bananas are enjoyed by birds but again, can be fattening, if fed too often. Do not feed any one fruit in excess. Cubed pieces of pear, apple, grape and melon may be given, plus berries, such as blackberries, raspberries and loganberries, cut in half.

Insects are very important for the insectivorous species and almost as necessary for other types too. Maggots should be cleaned thoroughly. Place them in an open container filled with bran. In two or three days they will have cleaned themselves thoroughly and the bran should be changed before they pupate into their first chrysalis. The maggots may be fed at any stage of their development cycle. In cool temperatures, the life cycle of the maggot slows down, but they should not be put under refrigeration, which stops them cleaning themselves. Mealworms should also be stored in bran which they eat. A culture may be set up quite easily or they may be purchased from pet food stores for convenience. They can also be fed to the birds during any stage of their life cycle. Make sure that the bran container has plenty of air by placing mesh over the top.

Locusts and crickets are another valuable food that may be purchased quite easily. The medium and larger softbills really enjoy these. Raw, minced meat, including beef, chicken and lamb, should be provided for the larger types. Do not let the meat go bad before being cleared away.

Hard boiled egg, mashed or finely chopped, is useful. Although not easily digested, it is very nutritious. Cheese may be given, cut into small cubes. It is useful in winter, helping birds to put on an extra layer of fat, but should be fed more sparingly in warm weather.

Stale bread crumbled into small pieces and soaked in milk is much appreciated. As with seedeaters, never use fresh bread as it is too indigestible.

The propagation of fruit fly larvae is acceptable in certain countries, but prohibited in others. If allowed, it is quite easy to breed these in a barrel of rotten fruit which should be kept at a warm temperature. This can be done in a garden shed. Fruit flies are useful for small species. In Australia, the soft body termites, known as white ants, are a most valuable source of food for softbills.

Commercially prepared mynah bird pellets are available at pet food stores. These are fed dry to the birds and were first developed for the mynah bird. However, even species as small as Pekin Robins eat and enjoy these. They are regarded by some fanciers as a lazy way of feeding softbills, but are very time-saving and do prevent many nutritional deficiencies. Many birds often prefer these to fruit and raw meat. The pellets contain several kinds of dried fruit, providing mineral value and trace elements for improved plumage. They also have a high protein content, lack heavy oils and are easy to digest.

Peanut butter is another useful extra which many softbills enjoy, although it may take some birds a little time to accept this addition. It is very nourishing and the easily digested oils are very good for plumage.

All dishes and drinkers used for softbills should be washed in boiling water each day. Once a bird has accepted a well balanced diet, it should not be changed or altered at random, but maintained. Each fancier learns the particular preferences of his birds and it is wise to keep to a routine, as most prove to be creatures of habit. All experts vary in their own preferences, but as a general rule, experimentation should be left to the more advanced aviculturist. The groups below suggest a suitable diet for each type of softbill.

OMNIVOROUS TYPES

This group includes: MYNAHS, STARLINGS and JAYS.

The menu should comprise mixed fruit accounting for almost half the daily ration, together with approximately 10% raw minced meat and 30% coarse grade insectile mix. They should also be given soaked bread or sponge cake daily and around 10% livefood. All these ingredients should be mixed together in one dish. Occasionally they may be given hard boiled egg as an additive. They should be offered plenty of plain boiled water to drink.

Also included in the omnivorous group are: BULBULS, TOUCANS, FAIRY BLUEBIRDS, FRUITSUCKERS and the many different species of TANAGERS.

These birds need about 25% more fruit than the above group. Coarse grade insectile mixture should makeup about 10% of their diet. Raw minced meat and soaked sponge cake or soaked bread should be given in the same amounts but only around 5% livefood is necessary. Again all the items are to be mixed in the same dish. A dish of nectar to drink is much appreciated and pure boiled water must always be provided.

FRUGIVOROUS TYPES

This group includes: CEDAR WAXWINGS and TOURACOS.

This group needs a large and varied amount of fruit. Coarse grade insectile mix should be sprinkled over the fruit to coat it well, encouraging the birds to eat this valuable item. About 10% raw minced meat should be given. Nectar powder may also be dusted over their fruit once a week or so, to add proteins, vitamins and minerals. The fruit itself is not sufficient to provide all the birds require. Boiled cubed potatoes, carrots and swedes may be added for a little more variety and extra vitamins and carbohydrates.

NECTIVOROUS TYPES

This group includes: SUGARBIRDS, IXULUS and YUHINAS.

The mainstay of the diet is nectar, forming about 60% of their food. Fruit is a very important ingredient and should make up a further 25%. Soaked bread or sponge cake may be added and they need about 5% raw minced meat. Drinkers should always be scrupulously clean so that the nectar is not spoiled or tainted. The fruit, meat and sponge cake or soaked bread should all be mixed together in one dish. In a separate dish, the birds should be given some fine grade insectile mixture to

which a few mealworms or maggots may be added. The insects should be coated in thick nectar, so that the insectile mix sticks to them. Avoid covering the heads, or they may die before being eaten. Fruit flies and an occasional spider are also enjoyed by these birds. Try to provide drinkers filled with plain boiled water, as some birds drink this as well as nectar.

INSECTIVOROUS TYPES

This group includes: INDIAN BLUE ROLLERS.

Coarse grade insectile mixture should be given to make up just under half the daily provision, plus about 15% mashed or chopped hard boiled egg, maggots around 20% and mealworms a further 15%. Add a little cheese, either cubed or grated, and the same amount of grated carrot, plus some small chunks of raw meat. Mix all ingredients together, sprinkling the egg, maggots and mealworms on top. To help tame these birds, insects may be offered by hand at times. It is a good idea to try and collect smooth caterpillars, crickets, blow-flies and spiders for feeding to birds. Some insectivorous species spurn mealworms and maggots since their normal prey moves faster, but try coating each maggot or mealworm with thick honey and some insectile mix to coax them to take these more readily. The heads must be left dry and uncoated or they may die before the birds eat them, especially mealworms.

CARNIVOROUS TYPES

This group includes: HORNBILLS.

The main requirement is raw meat in cubes, heavily coated with coarse grade insectile mixture. Half of the diet should be made up with dead, day old chicks which may be purchased from pet food stores, and the occasional dead mouse. Nectar powder should be dusted on to their foodstuff. Large locusts may be fed as a treat. In many ways their diet is similar to that of birds of prey. They also consume standard softbill fare, including fruit, soaked bread or sponge cake and cheese.

CHAPTER 3

BREEDING

AVICULTURISTS OFTEN START out with a collection of birds chosen for their colourful plumage or singing ability, without thought of breeding. Many keen fanciers later decide to expand their interest and attempt to breed their birds.

Successful breeding is achieved in six stages:

1 Courtship and display
The cock bird performs a ritual to attract his desired mate. He may show off his colourful plumage, dance around his hen, or sing. Once a hen responds and accepts a partner, mating takes place.

2 Nest site selection followed by nest construction and preparation.
Nest sites are chosen with care and both birds usually carry materials in their beaks and sometimes tucked under their wings to the site. The nest is lined with moss, feathers (often plucked from their breasts) and other soft material.

3 Egg laying and incubation
Once the hen begins to lay, the cock often feeds her, often on alternate days. He also stands guard at the entrance to the nest. One or both parents sit and incubate their eggs, keeping them at an even temperature while the embryos grow.

A ten-day-old Diamond Dove chick

Top: a nest site with plenty of cover encourages breeding

Above: a group of weaver nests

6 Juvenile moult when youngsters become independent

Young birds first moult when they are around three to four months old. They attain adult plumage and resemble their parents for the first time. They can now be considered able to fend for themselves. They should be closely observed to ensure that they are fit and healthy. This first moult is quite a strain on the body of young birds, and they can be lost suddenly and unexpectedly. This is particularly true of such birds as the Australian Gouldian Finch.

There are certain basic preparations that encourage birds to attempt to breed. A wide choice of nest boxes, baskets and other suitable receptacles should be made available for the birds to make their own selection. These facilities need to be well spaced out all over the accommodation. Some may be hung high up and others at different levels. Plenty of cover encourages the birds to investigate these potential nesting sites. Nesting materials may be placed in the aviary, such as grasses, hemp teasings, fine wool, mosses, small twigs and chicken feathers.

Many types of birds are stimulated into breeding condition by the amount of daylight available, while others choose to attempt to breed at any time of the year. Most birds choose spring as their breeding season. Plentiful supplies of food can be relied upon when the weather is good and insects are in good supply for the species which require them. It is always a wise idea to help birds into peak condition by feeding soaked and sprouted seeds or extra livefood demanded by the particular species as the breeding season approaches. Oats are a useful aid prior to the breeding season as they stimulate birds into breeding condition. Remove the oats once the hen has commenced sitting, or the cock bird may pester his hen with continuing advances.

Do make sure that the birds are protected from heavy rainfall and that nest sites are not too exposed, particularly to harsh winds. Some nest boxes and baskets should be hung in the shelter, as many birds prefer this additional security. Nest boxes and baskets should not be moved around once they have been positioned as this only confuses the birds. No tidying up

4 Chicks hatch and feeding and rearing commences

The young chicks are fed on regurgitated food supplied by their parents. Soft rearing food which is easily digested by the parents is of great help. Many birds also require insects to feed their young.

5 Chicks fledge and leave the nest

Once the chicks have grown a covering of feathers comprised of down and an outer covering of quills, they are ready to emerge from the nest for the first time. They usually return to the nest each night to roost. At this stage they are in juvenile plumage and are not fully independent. The parents may still feed them, although they are now largely capable of feeding themselves.

or cleaning of the flight should be contemplated at this time. Clean quarters are of course highly desirable and necessary, but the breeding season is the one time when this is not the first priority. The birds must feel secure and be disturbed as little as possible, if they are likely to be nesting and rearing a family.

It is soon evident when birds are interested in nesting. The cock birds perform their individual courtship rituals when interested in mating with their selected hens and the displays of many birds are amusing to observe.

Once the birds nest, the hens lay and incubation commences, keep any inspection of the nests to the absolute minimum. While some birds do not resent nest inspection, others will desert their nests at intrusion. If uncertain, leave well alone.

One of the problems most often encountered is that of chicks dying in the eggs before hatching, known as "dead-in-shell". This can be caused by a variety of factors: lack of humidity, dietary deficiencies or sometimes because the chick is unable to pierce the shell when it is time to hatch. Infertile eggs also account for a great many failures, particularly with young, inexperienced birds.

Some parent birds throw their young out of the nest the minute they hatch, cock birds being the usual offenders. This is also attributed to inexperience in most cases, as the parent bird does not realise they are chicks and treats them as foreign matter to be removed from the nest.

It is possible to determine whether eggs are fertile by holding them up to a strong light. An infertile or "clear" egg will be very light in weight, lack colour definition and actually appear hollow. A well filled egg is easily recognised.

Many large species, such as parrakeets, cockatiels and budgerigars, can be hand reared if necessary. An incubator or hospital cage is required. Hand rearing, although a time-consuming and tiring task, may be accomplished by those with patience. A temperature of 33°C (110°F) must be maintained for the chicks. A cardboard box, placed in a hospital cage, provides suitable housing. Paper tissues should be placed in the base of the box to absorb excrement.

The rearing mix should be made from milk and baby cereal in a thick consistency.

An eye dropper (or a syringe) may be used for feeding small chicks. Larger chicks may be fed with a teaspoon. The sides of the teaspoon should be bent upwards to facilitate the bird's easy swallowing of food. As chicks develop, the mixture should be gradually thickened. It is helpful to add finely grated cuttlefish bone and fine powdered bonemeal to the mix to help form strong, healthy bones and claws.

When hand rearing chicks, great care must be taken to avoid overloading the crop. It is easy to make the mistake of overfilling a chick's crop when using a syringe and a greedy bird often takes too much nourishment. When the crop appears overly distended, gentle massage often helps. All hand rearing tools should be warmed before use or chicks refuse to feed. Weaning should be accomplished by feeding soaked seed and soft fruits in most cases, using other foods for certain species.

Australian finches are not difficult birds to breed. However, there may be one or two problems when attempting to get them to make a start. If a young pair of birds shows no interest in building a nest, it may be that either the cock or the hen is not yet in breeding condition or that the pair is incompatible. Sometimes it helps to separate the pair for a few weeks and then re-introduce them to one another, possibly offering them a further selection of nest boxes or baskets. Existing sites should not be removed. If, however, there is still no activity, consider changing their partners.

If the hens lay eggs but fail to incubate,

A White Java
Sparrow at the nest

A Bengalese chick, just hatched, amongst a clutch of eggs

this usually indicates a feeling of insecurity. It may help to adjust the boxes slightly to admit more light to the entrance. Gouldian cock birds in particular often refuse to enter a dark hole. Alternatively, a little more cover may be needed around the site. Most changes however should be kept to an absolute minimum. In many cases where parents are young and inexperienced, chicks may hatch and their parents may feed them insufficiently or not at all. Young chicks may be lost occasionally.

Masked Grassfinches and other Australian finches consume large quantities of charcoal when breeding and should always be provided with a dish of charcoal. They spend a lot of time on the ground and must not be allowed to become chilled. If they roost with damp feathers prior to egg hatching, this dampness can help to soften

the egg shells for the young chicks to break out. But at other times it is not helpful since the parents can develop a cold.

Softbill breeding is easier to accomplish in a well planted aviary. Not only do these types require plenty of cover, but a good mixture of plants helps to encourage insects to inhabit the flight.

Many softbill species become pugnacious during the breeding season. Birds should be watched to make sure fighting does not take place and offenders may have to be segregated to their own quarters. Do not make it necessary for softbill pairs to have to compete for livefood by keeping too many birds together.

It may be worthwhile putting a compost heap in the aviary to provide a valuable source of small insects. Perhaps the most easy softbills to breed are the starling family, since their young will take maggots and small mealworms from a very early age. The provision of livefood is the most difficult requirement when breeding softbills.

Softbill chicks may also be hand reared in a hospital cage with a small pot of water covered with a piece of mesh for humidity. Very young chicks need feeding every hour from around 5 am in the morning to midnight, a somewhat daunting task. A week-old, medium sized softbill chick will require feeding every 1½ hours and a slightly older chick, every two hours. This is only to be recommended for the most dedicated fancier, although success in rearing a healthy chick, that might other-

A clutch of budgerigars eggs on a nest concave

wise have perished, makes all the necessary time and effort seem well worthwhile.

When dealing with birds that insist on producing young during winter months, it is necessary to provide twelve hours of light per day by means of artificial lighting so that parents may feed their chicks properly.

Most parrotlike birds are hole nesters and logs and boxes are their chosen nesting sites. They should also be supplied with bark and rotting wood. They appreciate plenty of humidity and in very warm weather, their nesting sites should be sprayed with a fine mist spray to help eggs hatch satisfactorily. This is best done from outside the aviary if possible.

With all breeding birds, always bear in mind that they need extra food when there are more mouths to feed, and increase quantities accordingly. As much soft food as possible should be given at this time. Parrotlike birds eagerly devour sweetcorn (maize) when rearing chicks and also enjoy it at other times. There are many types of soft food which may be given. Oatmeal porridge in medium consistency can be fed with crushed sunflower seeds (kernels only). Make sure, however, that the parents receive plenty of roughage. Green-food and mashed carrot will be very welcome, but do not overfeed. Wholemeal bread in small quantities moistened with honey and water is another popular standby. Try to vary the diet as much as possible and note which foods are taken with the greatest eagerness.

Crushed rusks, stale white or wholemeal bread, soaked in milk and fortified with mashed hard boiled egg, are very good for rearing chicks and ensure youngsters are plump and healthy. Most small seedeaters take this, as do both softbills and the larger seedeaters, including parrotlike birds already mentioned.

While the aviary should not be cleaned or tidied up more than is absolutely necessary during the breeding season, extra care should be taken to make certain that all feeding dishes and drinkers are completely clean. Scald all dishes and tubes in boiling water daily. Remove uneaten food well before it spoils. Prepare all feed in clean conditions and always wash your hands before preparation of the dishes, particularly if you have been using household sprays, insecticides or perfumed substances of any kind. These simple precautions may seem obvious but it is surprising how easy it is to forget when using substances that, though harmless to humans, may be toxic to birds. It is as well to observe the same precautions when feeding breeding birds as those employed for a human child.

Once birds have reared a maximum of two or three broods in a season, it is wise to segregate cocks from hens to prevent over-breeding, which only weakens the stock resulting in inferior young. Hens may be lost if they are allowed to breed too often. It is often difficult to replace a hen as there are often less hens for sale than cock birds. Many cock birds pine for a lost mate and refuse to accept a new substitute for some time, thus ruining a whole breeding programme. Many species like to use a nest box to roost in throughout the year, so segregating cocks and hens means that you can allow them to do this without having to worry about them going to nest. If preferred, remove nest boxes and baskets instead, and leave cocks and hens together, but the cocks may still indulge in mating activities and try and find other nesting places. Separation is generally considered best.

Do not allow birds to go to nest before they are at least eight months of age, or preferably a year old. Young hens can suffer from egg binding, when the bird is unable to expel the egg from the oviduct. It is painful, distressing and can kill the bird.

Split ringing birds for identification purposes is helpful, especially to record their age, as is a system of small indexed record cards detailing hatching dates and progress of the youngsters. This is a valuable asset for future breeding seasons, as well as a permanent record of the ages and history of birds. If breeding species such as canaries and budgerigars, which produce numbers of young each season, such a system is indispensable.

Many fanciers wish to ring their chicks with closed metal rings. It is normally advisable to do this if hoping to exhibit birds in shows in current year bred classes, since this proves that they are owner bred and is often a condition of entry. This entails removing the chicks from the nest. It should be done as quickly and carefully as possible. The age at which chicks are ringed varies according to their rate of

Above: a group of three-day-old budgerigar chicks in their normal cycle of hatching

Right: at six days old

Above: at eight days old

Right: at eleven days old

development. Gouldian Finches, for example, are usually ready between 10 and 12 days of age. Never try to ring a chick if the leg has grown too large. Rings for particular species are obtainable from specialist suppliers or cage bird societies. Rings should fit well but not be too tight. Holding the bird's leg gently, fold back the rear claw and slip the ring over the front claws. It may be eased on to the leg with a match stick which has been filed to a point. Only one leg is rung. Rings are coded with letters and numbers relating to the breeder's surname, registration number and the year.

Split plastic rings in various colours may also be used to identify birds for pairing up at a later stage. They are not acceptable for exhibiting purposes. These may be used at any age, since they fit on to any size of leg being pliable and open. There are sizes to fit all species.

Young budgerigars are always in great demand with pet stores that are eager to buy suitable birds for the pet trade. The well organised fancier can find a good outlet here for surplus stock which is not of a sufficiently high standard for exhibition. It is wise, of course, to keep the best birds if wishing to exhibit and breed top class birds.

It is important to maintain and, where possible, increase captive breeding. If not bred on a regular basis, species thought to be quite common can decline to a point where they become rare and expensive.

The keynote for success in breeding birds is patience. Do not worry unduly if your birds are slow in starting to breed. It is unwise to hastily sell pairs of birds and try others.

Give your birds time to settle down and adjust to their home. Feed them adequately at regular times and let them settle well and know that their home is a safe, secure and comfortable place before you expect too much from them. If they do not attempt to breed during their first season, they may well go to nest immediately the next season commences. Modify their quarters as little as possible unless the birds seem to be restless and insecure and always observe stock well before contemplating any major change.

Certain species are far more ready to breed and appear more domesticated than others. Try to start with the easy-to-breed species, then use that knowledge to help you breed the less willing types. Even the most experienced fanciers acknowledge that there is always something new to learn about breeding birds.

FOSTERING WITH BENGALESE

Bengalese are sometimes used to rear the chicks of Australian finches to increase the number of youngsters reared in a season. Eggs can be removed from a pair of Australian finches and placed under Bengalese, who then rear the chicks as their own. The pair of Australian finches then go on to produce more eggs.

Frequently, Bengalese are also used as foster parents for rearing chicks of those Australian finches who reject or refuse to feed their young.

There are one or two simple measures which are of great help if Bengalese are used as foster parents for rearing chicks of Australian finches. Always obtain the largest and strongest pair of Bengalese you can find. Colour is immaterial for this purpose, only their health and willingness to rear chicks are important. If possible, try and obtain a pair which have already proved themselves to be willing fosters.

It is vital that the Bengalese pair chosen is prepared to feed the youngsters properly. Before using these foster parents, try them with the chosen rearing food. If one or both of the birds only eat dry seed, do not use them and exchange them for another pair. A dry seed diet is not sufficient to rear healthy chicks. Test them first with a clutch of their own Bengalese youngsters to find out how well they rear chicks.

The young Bengalese may be split ringed for identification purposes and kept for future use. However, they should not be used to rear until they are at least eight months of age.

When fostering it is easier to provide more controlled conditions indoors than in an outside aviary. Whether inside or out, a fairly constant temperature of 20°C (68°F) is necessary to prevent the foster parents going into a moult during the rearing period, which would make them lose interest in feeding the young. Daily nest inspection should be performed when using Bengalese foster parents, so arrange the nest box in such a way that this is easily managed. Bengalese do not resent this as they are a thoroughly domesticated species. Do not allow perches to become fouled with droppings. If keeping indoors, use newspaper on the floor and change daily.

When ready to use the Bengalese, try to ensure that the fostered eggs or chicks coincide as closely as possible with the hatching of their own eggs. Their own incubation period is **14** days and chicks leave the nest after three weeks known as fledging. They do not object however if the fledging time of the foster chicks is different from their own. They do not have a specific nesting season and may go to nest at any time of the year.

When placing eggs under Bengalese, give no more than six at a time. As all the eggs hatch at the same time, chicks belonging to more than one pair of Australian finches cannot be identified with their parents once they have hatched. Try to keep accurate records as to how many clutches of eggs have been taken from each pair of Australian finches.

Most Australian finches will lay again eight or nine days after the last egg of the previous clutch is laid. If the eggs are taken away as soon as the last egg is laid, four or five clutches can be taken without overstraining the birds. A maximum of five clutches should be adhered to since inferior chicks result if any more are allowed.

As soon as the fostered chicks hatch, feed only sprouted seed which has been well washed and scalded for a few seconds in boiling water. Scalding removes some of the natural vitamins from the seed so it is beneficial to add two or three drops of a

multi-vitamin preparation to the birds' drinking water. Fresh rearing food with mashed hard boiled egg added should be offered daily. Always stick to the same proprietary brand, in case the Bengalese are reluctant to eat a new type once rearing has started.

As soon as the last chick leaves the nest, remove the nest box. This stops the Bengalese laying again before the young Australian finches can feed themselves properly. Do not replace the nest box until after the young finches have been removed.

Sometimes Bengalese prefer wicker baskets to nest boxes and it is a good idea to try them with both to see which they like best.

Australian finches may be reared in greater numbers by using Bengalese as foster parents, but it is generally considered that parent-reared chicks are stronger than their fostered counterparts. The choice may well be between quantity or quality. It is up to the individual fancier to decide which method is preferred and is the most practical. It is always useful to keep Bengalese for cases where parents are just not prepared to make the effort to rear their young or who desert while in the process.

In a mixed collection, it should be pointed out that Bengalese can make a nuisance of themselves by trying to assist birds who do not require their help. Bengalese are friendly and like to be involved with other birds' breeding chores. If housed with Zebra Finches they may even trade nests with them.

Certain shy types of finches sometimes desert their nests because of the intrusion of sociable Bengalese. It may be necessary to house them apart from other breeding birds at times, keeping them in reserve for emergencies.

A selection of closed metal rings for identification. Those shown fit a variety of different leg sizes.

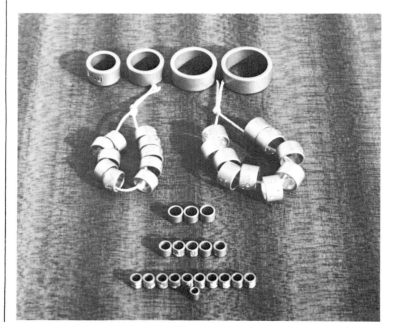

CHAPTER 4

AILMENTS

CAREFUL MANAGEMENT and feeding of birds ensures that illness is kept to a minimum, but there will be occasions when sickness is unavoidable. While some maladies are fairly simple to recognise and treat, there are many that are not. When in doubt, consult your local veterinary surgeon.

At the the first sign of illness, isolate the bird from its companions. Signs of illness may include the bird sitting with its feathers puffed up and generally looking out of sorts, very loose droppings, and often watery or half closed eyes.

The best treatment available for a sick bird is the prompt provision of heat. Reliable hospital cages may be purchased easily and the initial cost is soon recouped if these save the lives of just a couple of valuable birds. Most birds possess a body temperature of 32^{0}C (104^{0}F). As soon as a bird becomes ill, its body temperature drops drastically and this must be avoided at all costs. Energy is lost and food is refused.

Body heat must be restored as soon as possible. The hospital cage should be set at 24^{0}C (80^{0}F). Normally a mild antibiotic also helps, but care should be taken with any medicine since overdosing can prove fatal. Adequate food supplies and favoured tit-bits should be placed in the hospital cage to encourage the sick bird to eat. Plenty of boiled drinking water should be made available.

Reduce the temperature gradually when the bird shows active signs of recovery. The light in the hospital cage should be left on 24 hours a day to allow the bird to feed whenever it desires, building up its energy once more. Once the bird is eating well again, it is a sure sign that it is recovering, but it should not be allowed to rejoin the aviary until it is back to its normal self. A close watch should then be kept on the bird, in case of relapse.

When using your hospital cage make sure the perches are placed close to the floor or removed entirely, if the sick bird is not strong enough to perch. When the bird is able to grip again, they may be replaced. The bird's ability to perch properly again is another sign of improvement.

A number of the most common bird ailments are:

ABSCESS
Budgerigars and other parrotlike species often develop abscesses around the core or beak area. These may often be confused with tumours. They must only be removed by a veterinary surgeon and an antibiotic applied to prevent reinfection. They can be caused by bacterial agents.

ASPERGILLOSIS
This condition results from a lack of hygiene and is caused by the bird inhaling an airborne fungus called *Aspergillus fumigatus*. It occurs mostly in the larger kinds of parrotlike bird, but it can affect small parrakeets, although not usually budgerigars. Difficulty in breathing may be accompanied by a discharge from the bird's nostrils. Some fanciers add potassium iodine to their birds' drinking water ($2\frac{1}{2}$ grains to 4 tablespoons of water) as a preventative. If you suspect a new bird has this condition, consult your veterinary surgeon immediately.

ASTHMA
Asthma in birds is much the same as in humans, the symptoms being wheezing and heavy, laboured breathing. Symptoms may develop following a cold. Other causes of asthma include infection of the lungs and air sacs, aspergillosis (see above) and the inhalation of pollen or poisonous fumes. This condition may take several

months to eradicate. A bird with asthma will usually be seen to have a gaping beak and ruffled feathers. The bird's sinus passages often become clogged and treatment should consist of a decongestant cold remedy and a medium strength inhalant administered every day. These remedies may be purchased in the correct strength for birds from pet stores or supplied by a veterinary surgeon. Electric vaporizers may be used to ease the application of the inhalant. Parrakeets and budgerigars are the most likely types to suffer from this complaint. If the bird does not respond to treatment, consult your veterinary surgeon.

BACTERIAL INFECTION

Symptoms such as diarrhoea, loss of appetite and listlessness may indicate a bacterial infection. It should be prevented by good hygiene and a regular, thorough cleaning of the aviary with disinfectant. A new bird should be kept in isolation for a period of 30 days, before being placed in the aviary, to make sure it is not carrying any unpleasant virus. Always consult your veterinary surgeon if you suspect a bacterial infection.

BLEEDING

Bleeding from a wound must be stopped promptly with the use of a blood coagulant, such as Hydrogen Peroxide, applied with damp cotton wool.

BROKEN BONES

A broken wing is often the result of a night fright when a bird flies into something in the dark. A broken leg can be the result of a bird catching a leg in aviary netting. Most birds recover from these fairly easily on their own without any treatment. Broken wings however sometimes result in a permanent deformity which may affect a bird's flying ability. The bird should be placed in a hospital cage with its perch near the floor. The enforced idleness prevents the bird from using the affected part. Slings and splints are not always effective, but if desired, a splint can be made from lollipop sticks or feather quills. Prevention is far better than cure and all potential hazards should be eliminated from aviaries to minimise the risk of broken bones. Glass left without a wire covering is probably the single greatest danger, so make sure all glass is covered with netting.

Night frights sometimes cause birds to fly headlong into shelter walls or aviary wire, so lighting should be dimmed gradually. Try also to prevent predators from scaring the birds after dark.

BUMBLEFOOT

Finches and softbills sometimes suffer from this painful condition, particularly in old age. The feet become swollen and lumpy deposits resembling cheese appear on them. Since the treatment involves making small incisions in these substances and gently squeezing out the mass, it should be done extremely carefully if attempted at home. A blood coagulant should also be applied. It is more advisable to have this done by a veterinary surgeon, as it is very painful for the bird. Shock or heart failure could result if it is not done properly.

CANCER

Cancers in birds appear as lumps and may be visible or internal. While some external types may be removed, others are not treatable. In these cases it may be kinder to have the sufferer put painlessly to sleep. Always consult your veterinary surgeon if cancer is suspected.

CATARACTS

Scales forming across the eye may be caused by poor diet over a prolonged period of time. Little can be done for this condition, but always consult your veterinary surgeon.

COCCIDIOSIS

An uncommon disease caused by a microscopic organism called *Coccidia*. It affects the intestines. The bird becomes weak and emaciated and may have bloody diarrhoea. Sulphur drugs may be added to the drinking water, but it is difficult to cure and spreads alarmingly rapidly. It should not occur if good hygiene is practised; particular care is needed in hot weather. If suspected, consult your veterinary surgeon.

COLDS

Place the bird in a hospital cage at the first sign of a cold. The temperature should be set at 25°C (80°F). A bird with a cold sits with its feathers puffed out in a hunched position. The eyes may water and appear to be half closed. If severe catarrh is present, the bird opens and closes its beak frequently. Lack of appetite usually accompanies a cold. A mild cold remedy may be obtained from your pet store and an inhalant is also useful. A few vitamin drops and a little honey may be added to the drinking water to help restore a bird's energy.

CONJUNCTIVITIS
A painful eye inflammation caused by a virus, fungi, bacteria or some other irritant. An affected bird rubs its eye on a perch, blinks a great deal and there may be a watery or yellowish discharge from the eye. Prompt treatment by a veterinary surgeon with an antibiotic should cure the complaint.

CONSTIPATION
The bird will be seen to be straining and any droppings passed may be small, dry and hard. Greenfood and Vitamin B added to the drinking water help. Two tablespoons of black strap molasses mixed into a quart of distilled water and given to the bird to drink, also helps to alleviate this condition.

CROP IMPACTION
The crop can become blocked by food or as a result of a digestive disorder. A swelling appears on the lower neck and the bird appears to be trying to vomit. Surgery is usually necessary to remove the swelling so consult a veterinary surgeon for advice.

CYSTS
Yellow skin cysts, or non-malignant growths, often on the wings, are very common in budgerigars. They are easily removed by a veterinary surgeon.

DEAD-IN-SHELL
Many different factors may account for the chicks of breeding birds being found dead in their shells. One or both parents may be immature or too old. It may be caused by a genetic factor or dietary deficiency in certain vitamins and minerals, such as B and E group vitamins. Toxic substances may be responsible, such as DDT ingested by the parents at some time. The egg shell may be too thick or the chick stuck to the inner membrane. There may be a failure by the parents to incubate the egg properly or a lack of humidity. Try to establish the cause and if possible, rectify by appropriate measures.

DIARRHOEA
This condition is usually a symptom of other illness and is rarely caused by a diet problem. Two tablespoons of black strap molasses in a quart of distilled water may be given to the bird drink. If no improvement is noticed within a few days, consult your veterinary surgeon, since in rare cases, the bird may be suffering a serious illness, such as pneumonia or coccidiosis.

EGG BINDING
A very common problem, occurring frequently in young hens, and occasionally in mature hens. The bird is seen to be straining as though constipated. She is unable to expel the egg and once her strength is exhausted, death may quickly follow. The vent is puffy and swollen and the egg can be felt by touching around the area very gently with the forefinger. No pressure should be applied. Gentle bathing with warm water around the vent and a little warmth may help. This condition may be prevented by mixing a little cod liver oil with seed mixture for hardbills. Cold weather can also cause this problem, so hens should not be allowed to breed in particularly cold weather while they are young. Prevent the associated condition of soft shelled eggs by providing plenty of cuttlefish bone and grits. Inadequate diet, lack of calcium and exercise often give rise to both these conditions in mature hens. Always provide a mineral supplement for breeding birds.

EGG SAC RUPTURE
Rupture is caused when the hen expels not only the egg, but the egg sac membrane or oviduct as well. The egg must be gently forced through the opening and the membrane eased back into the vent, with a finger moistened with a saline solution to prevent infection of the delicate tissues.

ENTERITIS
Symptoms are inflammation of the small intestine normally accompanied by diarrhoea. Droppings are watery and often green. The bird seems to drink a great deal and eat large quantities of grit. The vent, or anus, is messy and the bird can be seen to be straining. Infectious enteritis is very dangerous and can destroy a whole aviary if the affected bird is not isolated at once. Overcrowding and dirty conditions are the

usual cause. New imports that have not been properly acclimatised may bring this infection with them, so never add a new bird to your stock without keeping it separate for as long as 30 days before introducing it to the aviary. If enteritis is present, it is usually evident within a week. The newcomer may not survive unless prompt treatment is given. The bird must be placed in a hospital cage and given a medication containing Sulfa Methazine. The hospital cage must be thoroughly disinfected after use.

FEATHER MITE AND QUILL MITE
Suspect mites when a bird's wings and tail look as though they have been chewed. A mild, gentle insecticide spray should eradicate the mites. Choose only a mite spray specifically designed for birds, easily purchased at pet stores.

FEATHER PLUCKING
Most feather plucking is performed by birds on their neighbours, although a bird suffering from boredom or desire for a mate often plucks itself. Some people feel a dietary deficiency may account for this tendency, but many other theories also abound on this subject. Sometimes a bully in the collection plucks the feathers of a weaker bird and may eventually make an attack to kill. Bullies should be removed and placed with larger birds, which deter a small dictator from taking such liberties.

FITS
Mynah birds are often subject to fits caused by improper diet and lack of exercise. Overexposure to the sun can also cause fits, not only in mynahs, but also in other species of tropical birds. It is essential to ensure that birds have adequate shade available in the aviary to escape the rays of hot sun.

FRENCH MOULT
If young birds, particularly budgerigars, show abnormal feather moult which persist even when they are mature, this condition is known as French moult. Wing and tail feathers continually moult. Overbreeding, incorrect feeding and perhaps an inherited factor are said to be the causes. It is better not to breed from such birds as no true cure exists.

GOING LIGHT
The term "going light" is applied to a sickly-looking bird that loses weight rapidly. It is a symptom, rather than a disease in itself, which may indicate a variety of other conditions. In extreme cases, it may mean that the bird has tuberculosis. Loss of appetite causes weight loss very rapidly. Death may result, so birds seen to exhibit this tendency should be isolated in a hospital cage and encouraged to start eating again as soon as possible. In some cases nothing seems to help and the bird dies. It is advisable to obtain a post mortem when this occurs in case another bird should suffer this condition. Identifying the problem may help to prevent a similar occurrence.

GOITRE
Goitre shows as a swelling on the neck. Only budgerigars, and usually only hens, suffer from this affliction. Incorrect functioning of the thyroid gland is the cause and can be brought on by breeding. Treatment with iodine blocks is the usual remedy. An affected hen must be removed from her mate to prevent breeding.

GOUT
The joints of legs, wings and neck are affected with a deposit of a hard white substance around the joints. It occurs rarely, and mainly in budgerigars and parrots, usually following a kidney infection. Massage under an anaesthetic is the normal treatment.

HEART DISEASE
Heart attacks usually prove fatal and occur mainly in older birds or birds that have a sudden shock or fright. Mild cases of heart disease may sometimes be helped by treatment with drugs obtainable only from a veterinary surgeon.

LICE
Lice sometimes appear on birds. Affected birds are restless, unable to settle, and scratch and rub their skin. Pyrethrum powder is very safe and effective for treating and ridding birds of these pests.

LIMBERNECK OR BOTULISM
Botulism is a deadly poison which gives rise to the condition known as "limberneck", a form of paralysis that starts in the

bird's neck and gradually affects the whole body. The organism is found in dirty water and rotten food that attracts flies. There is no cure, so an infected bird will die. Cleanliness is the best preventative.

MANGE MITE
Budgerigars and large parrakeets are sometimes affected by these mites. They affect beaks, ceres and other facial areas. Consult your veterinary surgeon, if mange mites are suspected.

MOULT
Birds moult twice a year, in spring and autumn, each moult normally lasting about six weeks. The bird loses certain feathers at a time. It is a natural occurrence, not an ailment, but it often causes problems. Birds look very scruffy during this phase. A careful watch should be kept and any bird that appears to be out of condition should be isolated and kept warm. Extra dietary supplements may be given to finches at this time and standard canary moulting food is very useful. Softbills should be given liquid vitamins and minerals added to their food; the best supplements come in powder form and sprinkle easily over their normal dishes. Any moult occurring outside spring or autumn, known as the "soft moult", may be the result of sun shining on a bird through glass, or of one bird being bullied by another.

NEPHRITIS
Inflammation of the kidneys is known as nephritis. This disease is common in all types of birds. The bird becomes listless, sits with ruffled feathers and drinks a lot of water. Droppings are white. If you suspect this disease, consult a veterinary surgeon.

ORNITHOSIS (Psittacosis)
Once a very dread disease since it was fatal, if contracted by humans. Thankfully it is no longer deadly, although it still causes very unpleasant pneumonia-like symptoms in humans and can make one seriously ill. But there are now very few cases in humans and less than there used to be in birds, due to the restrictions in bird imports and the regulations imposed to make conditions safer and healthier. It is a virus disease that causes lethargy, green diarrhoea, breathing difficulties and a discharge from eyes and nostrils. It is treatable if caught in time. Recovery is slow. It is usually found only in newly imported birds. If suspected, always consult a veterinary surgeon. Since it was once thought to occur only in Parrots, it was first named psittacosis, but as other species are now known to contract this disease, it is now called ornithosis.

OVERGROWN BEAK AND TOENAILS
Certain species exhibit a tendency towards overgrown toenails which can catch in aviary netting. It is quite easy to trim overgrown nails with fingernail clippers, taking care not to cut into the vein. If a vein is nipped inadvertently, stop the bleeding with Hydrogen Peroxide. The beak, if overgrown, may also be trimmed in the same way.

PNEUMONIA
An untreated cold may easily turn to pneumonia. Keep an affected bird warm, and swift treatment with Aureomycin or Sulfa Methaxine, obtainable from a veterinary surgeon, is important.

PSITTACOSIS – see ORNITHOSIS

RED MITE
Red mites are most prevalent during hot summer weather. Living in corners and crevices by day, they emerge at night to feed on the blood of birds. They can reduce a bird to a very anaemic state and even kill it. Pyrethrin is the safest standard aerosol exterminator of this pest, slower in effect than some other brands, but very safe for birds. It does not contaminate their food or water. South American softbills, when newly imported, often carry with them some unusual lice and mites and should be well sprayed before being introduced to the aviary.

REGURGITATION
Most birds regurgitate to feed their mates or young. Sometimes birds regurgitate to feed their favourite person as a sign of affection. Regurgitation for other reasons may denote illness, such as crop impaction, sour crop or mould. Simple indigestion or sometimes a cold, when the bird will regurgitate to bring up mucus, may cause this too.

RHEUMATISM

A painful swelling of the joints, which often occurs in older birds. Very little can be done to alleviate it, although massage can sometimes help.

RICKETS

This can occur in many birds, but particularly in young budgerigars. Incorrect diet, deficient in Vitamin D, causes the bird to have short, badly shaped legs with swollen joints. The bird is weak and unable to fly. Bone meal and Vitamin D3 should be added to the feed.

SALMONELLOSIS

This is caused by Salmonella bacteria. It is often fatal to birds and can be transmitted to human beings. The symptoms include lethargy, diarrhoea, dysentery and excessive thirst. Convulsions normally occur followed by sudden death. If suspected, the bird's droppings should be analysed. Early treatment with the correct antibiotics from a veterinary surgeon will normally cure it. The bird's quarters must then be thoroughly disinfected.

SCALY FACE AND SCALY LEG

This condition is caused by a small mite. Yellowish-white crusts form on the beak, around the cere and eyes, and sometimes on the legs and around the vent. Treat with a 10% solution of Benzyl Benzoate applied with cotton wool every day for a week. Prompt treatment should be given, as severe cases can lead to deformity of the beak.

SHOCK

Shock may be caused by a number of factors. Rough handling is the most frequent cause, so care must always be taken in catching birds and in their handling. Night frights too can cause shock and may lead to a heart attack.

SINUS DISORDER

Sinus problems often appear after a cold. They are easy to identify since the bird has clogged nostrils and watering eyes. A badly impacted sinus often creates a large swollen nodule of hard mucus substance. The nodule must be lanced by pricking with a sterilised needle. A scab forms and is later easily removed by gentle massage. Gently work off all the hard mucus with damp cotton wool or a cotton bud to prevent re-occurrence of this condition.

SOFT-SHELLED EGGS

This is often caused by a calcium deficiency. It seems to occur more often in budgerigars than in other other species. Many fanciers use Calcium Boroglucanate administered directly or in drinking water to prevent their birds producing soft-shelled eggs.

SORE FEET

Birds sometimes get sore feet if seed husks and droppings get stuck to them. The resulting irritation causes little sores to form. The feet must be dipped in warm water mixed with mild disinfectant and the hard lumps gently washed off. Gently towel dry the feet and lightly apply some Vaseline, making sure it is absorbed. The bird should be treated several times if necessary.

SOUR CROP

Sour crop is caused by a digestive upset and can result in a strong, unpleasant smell emanating from the afflicted bird. A teaspoon of baking soda should be mixed into a quart of water and given to the bird over a period of two days to cure the problem.

SWOLLEN OIL GLAND

The oil gland is located at the base of the tail and contains oil used in preening and grooming. Sometimes the oil clogs up the gland and a swelling is caused. The gland is sore and inflamed. A toothpick, matchstick or damp cotton wool bud should be used to remove the offending material with very gentle pressure.

WORMS

Worms occur more often in parrotlike species than in other birds. There are several different types. Cleanliness is the best method of prevention. Always consult your veterinary surgeon, if worms are suspected, who will prescribe a proprietary brand worming product.

CHAPTER 5

EXHIBITING AND PHOTOGRAPHING BIRDS

EXHIBITING

An interesting way to expand the hobby of bird keeping is to join a club and exhibit birds in shows. In most countries there are specialist societies and caged bird clubs, who offer their members help in such matters as bird management, breeding and exhibiting in shows.

Most shows vary in duration between one and three days. Open shows allow all to enter, including those fanciers who are not members of a club. Invitation shows encourage entry from several clubs, and annual shows are staged by bird clubs for their members only. Depending on the type of club, the birds featured may be of all varieties, such as budgerigars, canaries, Zebra, Bengalese, exotic seedeaters and softbills, or just one type of bird. There are also young stock shows following the breeding season, which are fairly small events. Pairs table shows, where birds are entered in couples, are also small events.

Fanciers are often in doubt as to how to exhibit or stage their birds, and wonder if their stock is good enough for the show bench. Joining a local club can be of great value, for not only is it be possible to see other exhibitors' birds and gauge the standard required, but more experienced fanciers are often only too pleased to help and advise a newcomer.

Various types of show cage are needed for the exhibition of particular species. There are certain set standard sizes and colours in show cages. Take, for example, standard softbill show cages. These are quite large in size and painted in black gloss paint on the outside and white gloss paint on the inside. The bars may be painted in black to give a good view of the exhibit, although white painted bars are allowed.

Cages should always be kept spotlessly clean as points may be lost for a dirty cage. Paint should be re-touched when necessary.

A bench of exhibition Gouldian Finches in their show cages

Medium and small softbill show cages are normally decorated, preferably with natural materials such as mosses, bark and ferns. An attractive landscaped effect may be created to show the species off to advantage. Pay attention to the colours of materials used, so that an attractive blend between the colour of the bird and the background is achieved. The wire front of the show cage may easily be removed to allow decoration. This should not be done too many hours before the show or the plants may wilt before judging. It is wise not to overdo the decoration as a crowded show cage may distract the eye of the judge from the exhibit itself. If the decoration is in keeping with the bird's natural habitat, so much the better. The larger species of softbill, such as jays, mynahs and similar birds, should not have their show cages decorated as they usually wreck the display.

Cage floors should be covered with absorbent blotting paper, white being the colour most often used. Some fanciers choose a colour which tones in with the bird's plumage and this can draw the eye to a bird very successfully.

Budgerigar and canary show cages both have a standard design, size and colour. They are never decorated and there are quite strict rules governing this section of the bird fancy, in both cases. Exotic types of seedeaters should not have their show cages decorated, but dowel perching may be exchanged for natural twigs. The floor of the exotic seedeater's show cage is usually covered with its seed for convenience of feeding.

Most show cages are sold complete with a drinking pot. In exotic softbill show cages it is necessary to install a drinking tube, particularly for the nectar feeders.

Show entry forms with a schedule of the various classes are obtained from the show secretary of the club staging the event. He or she is also able to advise how to complete the form correctly. This, again, is where membership of a club is a distinct advantage.

Once the entry form is received by the show secretary, the exhibitor is sent numbered labels to affix to the show cage for identification. Enclosed with these there is usually a lifting card for listing the cage and class numbers. After the show, birds are checked out against this lifting card. On show day a certain number of stewards are on duty to assist the judges and to check birds in and out of the show. They also make sure that all the exhibits are regularly given water and food as required. The stewards are there to take care of the birds and to make sure they are secure. They also usually attend to such duties as pinning rosettes on the winning exhibits' cages.

Never put any distinguishing marks on show cages, nor name and address labels. This is not allowed and an entry marked in this way is sure to be disqualified.

Some specialist societies have stricter rules than those in most general use and these should always be studied carefully before entering a show. In order to qualify for specialist society awards, known as "specials", it is necessary to be a full member of the particular society concerned. In open shows, the awards are available for any entrant to win.

In Current Year Bred classes for young birds bred by the exhibitor, many clubs rule that birds must be wearing closed rings to prove that they are truly owner bred. A closed ring bears the breeder's surname, initial and registration number. Split plastic rings used for identification purposes are not acceptable.

On show day a catalogue of the entrants in all the classes is produced and the results

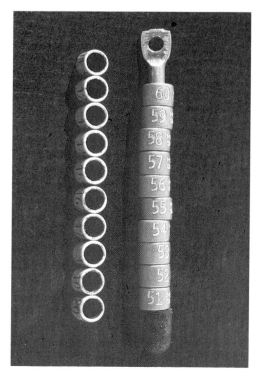

Closed metal rings used to fit budgerigars

of the judging are added on a printed sheet after the judging has been completed.

Birds are usually awarded class places ranging from 1st to 7th. Winners of classes are eligible to compete for the special awards such as Best Seedeater, Best Parrotlike, Best Softbill, Best Canary, Best Budgerigar, Best Zebra and Best Bengalese, to name a few. The most coveted award of many shows is Best Bird in the Show. In canary and budgerigar shows the awards are more complex and diverse. Award titles often vary from show to show, but all are much sought after by the keen exhibitor, and the rosettes, cups and plaques that are awarded are much prized. Usually the financial gain is quite small, although there are often cash specials too.

The seedeating classes often offer specials for Best Common, Best Rare Seedeater and Best Australian. A really good quality seedeater can go on to win Best in the Show, beating quite dazzling softbills. Do not feel that a really expensive or unusual bird is the only way to take top honours.

When showing canaries, begin by entering birds in the novice class for a particular breed of canary. Make sure that the correct type of show cage has been purchased for the canary, whether it be Yorkshire, Border, Gloster or one of the lesser known varieties or mules (a cross between a canary and a finch).

Ensure when completing entry forms that birds are entered in their correct classes, as "wrong classed" birds are normally disqualified from competition. This applies to nearly all sections, although, in practice, may be waived where exotics are concerned.

Many canary fanciers hand wash their birds in preparation for a show, often with an old fashioned shaving brush and lather. The bird is rinsed off with warm water and thoroughly dried afterwards. This can, however, take a great deal of oil out of the bird's feathers causing the plumage to lose its sheen. Therefore, some fanciers prefer to allow their birds to bathe or may spray them with warm water from a fine mist spray.

Canaries, in common with other types of birds, should be given training in a show cage before being exhibited, so that they are used to its confines and are steady and confident before the judge. No bird should ever be shown unless it is fit. It is useful to have a substitute available when entering birds for show, just in case the proposed exhibit falls ill on the day.

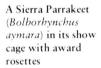

A Sierra Parrakeet (*Bolborbynchus aymara*) in its show cage with award rosettes

Budgerigar exhibitors are divided into four categories: Beginner, Novice, Intermediate and Champion. A certain number of wins as a "beginner" entitles a move to the higher grade of "novice". Competion becomes fiercer in the higher grades. Budgerigars that win consistently on the show bench can become very valuable.

There is no such thing as an ideal budgerigar. Each judge has his own idea of the perfect bird, and the diversity of size and shape, especially with regard to the head, is quite pronounced. This is possibly the most difficult section in exhibiting and the rules are very strict with regard to certain points, particularly the spots on the area around the chin, known as the mask.

Zebra Finches and Bengalese are always shown in pairs. Matching of physical characteristics within the pair is important: choose birds of the same size and colour.

While the preparation of exotic softbills may be a little more difficult, particularly with soft feathered birds, in general terms the rules are not quite so strictly defined. Small seedeaters are easier to stage, so they are a good choice for the beginner. Spray plumage with a fine mist spray of warm water for a few days before the show for a glossy finish.

Parrotlike birds usually show well and confidently. A nicely matched pair or a single specimen may be staged. A few sprays with warm water add a fine sheen to the plumage. Some fanciers add vitamin preparations to their birds' drinking water prior to and during the show season, although this is not essential if birds are in good health.

It is important to give birds as much rest as possible between shows, so do not enter too many competitions. Give birds extra nourishment on returning from a show, such as their favourite tit-bits or honey added to their drinking water. Do not place the birds outside without making sure that they are re-acclimatised, especially in cold weather.

While transporting, show cages may be carried in travelling boxes or covered in material to prevent draughts.

At all times the health and well being of the birds should be given priority. Make sure that birds are steady and calm enough for staging and do not show any birds that display signs of undue stress.

PHOTOGRAPHING

Photographing birds is another very enjoyable and rewarding activity for the fancier, with endless possibilities to investigate.

The amateur often begins with black and white photography, perhaps even learning to develop and process the results at home. Some dramatic shots may be achieved by using black and white film, particularly when photographing waterfowl species. Many species of swan, goose, duck and moorhen photographed on water make attractive and eye catching photographs.

The 35mm format is usually the most suitable for amateur photography, and professional processing laboratories provide a reasonable service. It is worth shopping around to compare prices and quality.

Colour slides generally have better definition than prints taken on negative film. Colour slides, or transparencies as they are also known, are usually mounted in either cardboard or plastic. They may be viewed with a projector on a screen, or in a small hand or table top viewer, or on a light box. It is even possible to have video films made up from slides. Slides can be mounted at home, as the transparencies slip easily into the mounts. This does save the accumulation of large numbers of mounted slides containing some reject shots, which may create storage problems. When sending a film for processing, always specify "mounted" or "unmounted" for slides, as there is often a small price difference. Always choose good quality film for photography and do not be tempted to use outdated materials.

Whether photographing birds at home or in other locations, it is necessary to purchase a certain amount of specialist camera equipment. A 35 mm camera with a standard 50 mm F1.8 lens is a good start, and then decide on additional lenses to compliment the equipment. One of the most useful lenses for bird photography is a zoom lens of a suggested range of either 75 mm to 150 mm or 80 mm to 210 mm. The maximum aperture may vary between F4 and F5.6. You may then choose either a 300 mm F5.6 or perhaps a cadioptric mirror lens of 500 mm F8, which covers the need to photograph small birds at a distance. While cadioptric lenses are more expensive, they are lighter and more compact to use than normal fixed focal length lenses. They also eliminate the need

Moorhens under a
weeping willow in a
large aviary

to use a tripod for steadying the camera. A hand held shot taken with a 300 mm lens will often exhibit signs of camera shake, particularly in low light situations. Wide angle zoom lenses between 24 mm and 35 mm F4 are very useful for taking photographs of large aviaries or scenic views of birds in pool or countryside settings.

There is a great variety of lenses to choose from, but it is easier to buy zoom lenses which cover a wide range of focal lengths, rather than to have to carry around a lot of equipment. A tripod is a valuable asset in difficult lighting conditions and should not be too expensive. You can also purchase a device called a teleconverter, which multiplies the focal lengths of the lenses you already have, and saves the additional expense of buying several extra lenses, although quality may be reduced. A good quality flashgun is also useful and it may even be worth buying filters for special effects.

A library of colour slides of birds gives great enjoyment. Consider giving slide shows at bird club meetings, clubs for old people or in schools and colleges, or entering photographs in competitions such as those run by photographic magazines. If the collection is really expert, photo libraries may buy sets of top quality slides or represent the photographer as an agent on a commission basis.

When photographing birds from outside an aviary, the main difficulty is to minimise the effect of wire netting. Experiment with the aperture setting until the wire is no longer prominent in the viewfinder. It often helps to focus a little below the subject. Practice soon reveals how best to achieve the desired shot without the wire being obtrusive.

Patience is vital in bird photography. It is worth waiting for just the right moment when the bird has settled and is not aware of an interested presence. A hasty shot often results in a blurred image of little use.

Photographing birds in the aviary can be a source of great pleasure. It is surprising how soon they become accustomed to the

Above: Pelicans make amusing subjects in large enclosures and are usually tame

Right: unusual angles of photography give added interest, as in this shot of a pelican with its gannet companion

camera, often becoming quite "stage struck", immediately adopting a pose as their owner approaches.

Photographing small birds can pose a few problems. Some fanciers construct a special box type cage with a removable wire front, or else a show cage can be used to good effect. Different coloured backgrounds can be created by using coloured blotting paper. Twig perches provide a more natural setting. When using this type of box, give birds time to settle and wait until they are calm and still. When using flash for indoor work, a little extra care is necessary so that birds are not alarmed. They soon get used to flash photography and are not too startled by the sudden light.

Make sure that the background is tidy when photographing birds, and try to ensure that the subject is not obscured by twigs or branches in the foreground. It is difficult to frame a shot of a bird in dense foliage. Always give the bird a little time in the hope that it will move to a more visible position.

Some bird gardens may be prepared to give permission to photograph "behind the

Top: a Cattle Egret in sentry-like pose

Left: a dignified Eagle Owl

Above: an unusual-looking King Vulture for the specialist bird keeper

scenes" and allow entry to certain areas, but never during the breeding season.

In the first instance, try photographing the larger species. Birds of prey are usually excellent subjects. The King Vulture is a colourful bird of prey which can look both imposing and comical. Owls always seem to come out well in photographs. During the day, when they slumber fitfully opening their eyes every now and then, they can be photographed with ease. The Snowy Owl is particularly photogenic.

Macaws, cockatoos and large parrots are interesting to photograph. Macaws can often be viewed at liberty in bird gardens and zoos and are usually very tame, often striking engaging poses with nuts, fruit or seeds clutched in one foot as they feed. Their preening habits also make notable photographs, particularly when one bird grooms a mate or companion.

The hues of such parrots as the Eclectus Hen, which is bright carmine red and purple, make colour film a must. Flamingoes make a pleasing spectacle, particularly when in an attractive pool setting and Toco Toucans and other members of the toucan family provide a chance to take an arresting picture. A

favourite shot of many photographers is the splendour of the Indian Peacock with its tail fanned out in spectacular display.

Hornbills such as the Red-Billed Hornbill, cranes, storks and large softbills such as touracos, are all full of potential for amateur photographers. Avocets and stilts and many similar species are often seen in zoos in marine-like settings which can look pleasing. It may be preferable to photograph them in their natural environment, if such an opportunity arises.

A day photographing birds can make a really interesting outing for the whole family, and children particularly enjoy zoos and bird gardens. The combination of children, birds and animals can produce prize winning shots often published by newspapers.

Do not be too upset if first attempts produce a number of failures, and be prepared to experiment. One good photograph is worth a great many practice efforts. A framed enlargement of a magnificent photograph makes it all seem worthwhile!

A colourful Laminated
Hill Toucan

Below: an Oyster
Catcher investigates an
old rowing boat

HOW TO SELECT COMPATIBLE BIRDS

BEFORE PURCHASING BIRDS, it is a good idea to visit some bird gardens, zoos and private aviaries to look at their healthy specimens. Compare the different types and observe their behaviour closely.

The choice of dealer is most important when buying birds. Check up on as many different sources as possible, as pet stores vary tremendously in the quality and selection of birds on offer. Do try to take as much time as possible over this. It is often better to wait a little longer for the birds of your choice, rather than to buy inferior stock. It may also be possible to obtain birds from experienced fanciers who wish to sell their surplus stock.

There are some basic points to watch for when trying to select healthy birds:

1 Make sure the bird is not sitting huddled up with feathers puffed out.
2 Ensure that eyes are clear and open, showing no signs of watery discharge.
3 Check vent to make sure it is clean and unsoiled. It should not appear to be damp.
4 Make sure that the legs and feet are undamaged and that toe nails are intact.
5 Examine nostrils to see that they are clear and free from discharge.
6 Feel the breast bone of larger birds to see that there is a fair amount of flesh on the breast.

Do not worry unduly about the appearance of the plumage. Moulting birds often look quite scruffy, as do those that are feather plucked or have had wings clipped by dealers or exporters. Parrotlike species often have their wings clipped to prevent escape. Feathers soon grow again and a bath often makes a bird look much better. The only point to remember when purchasing a moulting bird is that its general health may be a little under par at this time and extra nourishment may be required. Some birds, however, go through a moult without difficulty. No hard and fast rule can be applied here, so if in doubt always provide extras to the normal diet. (See Chapter 2, ''FEEDING'').

When trying to choose a true pair of birds of a species where no sexual differences are visible or described, it is advisable to purchase several birds and allow them to pair up. This usually results in at least one true pair and the surplus may then be sold or exchanged.

When purchasing birds, note that very healthy specimens often sit balanced on one foot while perching or roosting. This is usually a good sign, although some healthy birds resolutely perch on both feet. A bird that is seen to be busily preening its feathers is generally a fit bird, interested in its appearance and in reasonable health. If a bird is at the feeding dish, look for signs of a healthy appetite. Avoid a bird that appears to be gorging itself on grit, as this is not a good sign. Grit is used to masticate food in the crop, before digestion. Too much grit indicates a poor or sluggish digestion. In general, choose a bird which appears fairly lively and interested in its surroundings.

Keep new birds in separate cages in the bird room or shelter for a short period before releasing them into an outside aviary. Remember to acclimatise birds that are to live outside. They should not be transferred from an indoor site to an immediate drop in temperature, although this need not be a problem if the weather is warm or if the bird has come from another outside location.

When choosing birds it is important to select only those which are compatible and can live together in harmony. Incompatible birds fight over favourite perching spots, nesting sites and feeding dishes. Unhappy birds refuse to breed and, in extreme cases, severe injuries, such as damaged toes or the loss of an eye, can be caused, particularly amongst the parrotlike species.

The guide list on the next page suggests eight "compatability" groups. The birds in each group live happily together without aggression, ensuring that some of the more unfortunate mixtures are avoided.

It must be emphasised that these groups are a guide only – always remember that there are individual birds who may have aggressive tendencies. Watch out for bullies in the collection and isolate individuals where necessary. It is often better to sell such a bird, rather than to wait and hope it may change its ways. Sometimes, however, the addition of another dominant type may alter the situation.

In some cases, it may be possible to mix birds that are not listed in these groups. Individual temperaments in birds vary, as they do in humans, and there are always exceptions to the rule. However it is best to leave experimentation to the more experienced fancier who has a spacious aviary and plenty of time to devote to watching his birds for signs of aggression. If in doubt, do not house the birds in question in the same aviary. It is always a good idea to consult your local bird club, dealer or an experienced fancier for advice.

Each group has a symbol for quick reference. Chapter 7 describes each bird mentioned in these lists in detail, with notes on size, physical characteristics, diet and breeding. The birds described have been chosen, not only for their compatibility with other birds within a mixed collection, but also because they are widely available. Each bird in Chapter 7 is illustrated for ease of recognition, and is coded with the symbols of the group, or in many cases, the groups, to which it belongs.

It is a good idea for the novice bird keeper to start his collection with seedeaters, possibly moving on to the more difficult to manage softbill species at a later stage.

The most easily managed species of seedeaters are birds, such as the Zebra Finch, Bengalese and many of the small waxbills. Australian Grassfinches, while relatively easy to care for with regard to feeding, may need extra warmth. Budgeri-

gars, cockatiels and small parrakeets, such as Bourke's Parrakeet, are very simple to care for and an excellent choice.

Where parrotlike birds are concerned, very few species may be kept together with any degree of safety at all, unless in a very large aviary. If in doubt, do not keep the species in question together. Some parrotlike birds attempt to murder each other without the slightest provocation, and may spitefully nip at toes and eyes. Only the species mentioned in Group 4 should be mixed sparingly in as much space as possible. Do not be tempted to try and house any of the lovebird species in a mixed collection. They may look small and beautiful, but their sharp, curved beaks can be lethal. They should only be kept in pairs in individual housing. The Fischer's Lovebird is the only species which may safely be kept in a colony of its own breed. Never put lovebirds in with finches for they will certainly attack.

The same warning applies to all the small species of parrot, such parrakeets as conures and all the nectar feeding parrakeets. However, hanging parrots may be kept with their own kind and with large tanagers, if the aviary is densely planted and extra care and caution are taken. Since hanging parrots are quite popular, they are covered in Chapter 8.

Some fanciers succeed in keeping seemingly odd selections, which thrive together. Birds which are introduced to their accommodation all at the same time often agree better than those introduced separately. Certain factors may assist the newcomer in avoiding the more basic errors.

The size of the aviary or accommodation provided has a considerable influence on the success of mixing various species. Birds are always less tolerant of one another in a small enclosure than in a larger area, as they are territorial creatures who like to claim the largest spot for themselves. It is sound common sense to give them as much space as possible.

Smaller birds are content with a smaller area for their own preserve than the larger species. Breeding pairs must be alloted more space than single specimens. If there is very little space available, consider keeping only single cock birds of individual species. In this way, it is possible to house a colourful collection of attractive birds without risk of fighting in a small flight. Many fanciers who do not wish to breed their birds obtain great enjoyment from managing a collection of lone cock birds selected for either their colourful plumage or pleasant singing ability.

Some birds prefer densely planted aviaries, which provide the best cover for nest building and privacy for the more timid and shy birds. Remember that preparing food for softbills is time-consuming compared to the simple feeding requirements of seedeaters. If keeping birds, such as the Chinese Painted Quail and other ground species, take care not to tread on their eggs or young when entering the aviary.

Providing several roosting spots, nesting sites and feeding dishes prevents arguments between birds, so try to offer as much choice as possible. Too few roosting spots or nesting sites in the accommodation means fighting can break out even amongst the most placid birds. Nest boxes and baskets should be placed as far apart as possible and evenly distributed around the quarters.

When introducing new birds of any kind to a mixed collection, it is useful to provide an extra place for the new birds to feed, so that they do not interfere with the usual feeding routine of the established birds. This often prevents fighting.

It is quite easy to keep birds of similar size and habits together. If a smaller type is introduced to the collection it is likely to be bullied, likewise if a larger type is

COMPATIBILITY GROUPS

GROUP 1 ●	GROUP 2 ○	GROUP 3 ▨	GROUP 4 ☐
Red Avadavat	Red Avadavat	Bengalese	Budgerigar
Bengalese	Bengalese	Bicheno	Cockatiel
Bicheno	Bicheno	Canary	Laughing Dove
Vinaceous Fire Finch	Chestnut-Breasted	Chestnut-Breasted	Bourk's Parrakeet
Green Singing Finch	Finch	Finch	Elegant Grass
Lavender Finch	Diamond Sparrow	Diamond Sparrow	Parrakeet
Chinese Painted	Diamond Dove	Diamond Dove	Plum-Headed
Quail	Vinaceous Fire	Goldfinch	Parrakeet
African Silverbill	Finch	Gouldian Finch	Red-Rumped
Spice Bird	Gouldian Finch	Long-Tailed/	Parrakeet
Star Finch	Long-Tailed/	Heck's Grassfinch	Splendid Grass
Green Twinspot	Heck's Grassfinch	Masked Grassfinch	Parrakeet
Peter's Twinspot	Masked Grassfinch	Green Singing	Turquoisine Grass
Cordon Bleu	Green Singing	Finch	Parrakeet
Waxbill	Finch	Black-Headed	California Quail
Golden-Breasted	Black-Headed	Mannikin	
Waxbill	Mannikin	White-Headed	
Red-Eared Waxbill	White-Headed	Mannikin	
Orange-Cheeked	Mannikin	Pin-Tailed Parrot	
Waxbill	Pin-Tailed Parrot	Finch	
Violet-Eared	Finch	Parson Finch	
Waxbill	Parson Finch	Chinese Painted	
Zebra Finch	Chinese Painted	Quail	
Indian Zosterops	Quail	African Silverbill	
	Red-Billed Quelea	Spice Bird	
	Spice Bird	Star Finch	
	Star Finch	Green Twinspot	
	Green Twinspot	Peter's Twinspot	
	Peter's Twinspot	Paradise Whydah	
	Cordon Bleu	Zebra Finch	
	Waxbill		
	Violet-Eared		
	Waxbill		
	Paradise Whydah		
	Zebra Finch		

brought in it often tries to dominate the rest. Try to avoid such practices.

In their natural state, birds operate a "pecking order": the stronger dominate and rule the weaker. This order is often observed in a captive collection and when a newcomer is introduced it is certainly noticed. Such encounters are best kept to a minimum and should be watched closely. In a few days, the normal order should be restored and the new bird or birds accepted. A newcomer is usually subservient or sometimes on equal terms, but in some cases, exerts its own brand of authority. Large omnivorous birds and insect eating species should only be kept together when they are of similar size, strength and habit.

Specialised bird collections can be a source of great interest, particularly those based on a particular theme, such as a geographical location: Africa, India or Asia, Australia or South America. Birds from these countries have interesting feeding habits, colours, shapes and territorial behaviour patterns which may be observed and even seriously studied in an amateur collection. Another possibility is to purchase a collection of all-white strains from another aviculturist; this makes a very attractive and unusual aviary. Many of these can be kept in one suitable sized aviary and might include a Zebra Finch, a Bengalese Finch, some species of quail, a Java Sparrow, a White Dove, a pigeon and a canary. White budgerigars are quite common, but they are not usually suitable companions for other small species.

COMPATIBILITY GROUPS (continued)

GROUP 5 ◄	GROUP 6 ◇	GROUP 7 ◆	GROUP 8 △
Budgerigar	Canary	Black-Crested Bulbul	Asian Fairy Blue Bird
Green Cardinal	Green Cardinal	Yellow-Collared Ixulus	Golden-Fronted Fruitsucker (a single bird only, pairs are too aggressive)
Pope Cardinal	Pope Cardinal	Andaman Mynah	Pileated Jay
Red-Crested Cardinal	Red-Crested Cardinal	Pagoda Mynah	White-Crested Laughing Thrush
Cut-Throat Finch	Goldfinch	Rothschild's Mynah	Andaman Mynah
Laughing Dove	Japanese Hawfinch	Pekin Robin	Pagoda Mynah
Japanese Hawfinch	Java Sparrow	Indian Blue Roller	Rothschild's Mynah
Java Sparrow	Magpie Mannikin	Purple Sugarbird	Indian Blue Roller
Magpie Mannikin	Pekin Robin	Yellow-Winged Sugarbird	Superb Spreo Starling (a single bird only, pairs are too aggressive)
California Quail	Red-Billed Quelea	Blue-Capped Tanager	Cedar Waxwing
Red-Billed Quelea	Napolean Weaver	Emerald-Spotted Tanager	
Napolean Weaver	Yellow-Backed Whydah	Cedar Waxwing	
Paradise Whydah	Yellow Sparrow	Black-Chinned Yuhina	
Yellow-Backed Whydah		Indian Zosterops	
Yellow Sparrow			

CHAPTER 7

SUITABLE SPECIES FOR A MIXED COLLECTION

EACH OF THE BIRDS in this chapter is suitable for inclusion in a mixed collection. The 71 birds described fit into eight groups, as listed in Chapter 6. The description of each bird carries a symbol or symbols relevant to its group or groups. Careful reference to these symbols prevents the fancier from mixing unsuitable types in an aviary.

Whilst the species described in this chapter live contentedly with selected companions, always watch for individual birds with difficult temperaments, and remove any such specimens from the aviary at the first sign of trouble.

It may also be possible to mix birds of species not mentioned in this chapter, depending on the conditions in the aviary and the individual natures of the birds involved. However, the species described in this chapter are known to be good "mixers" and are usually readily available.

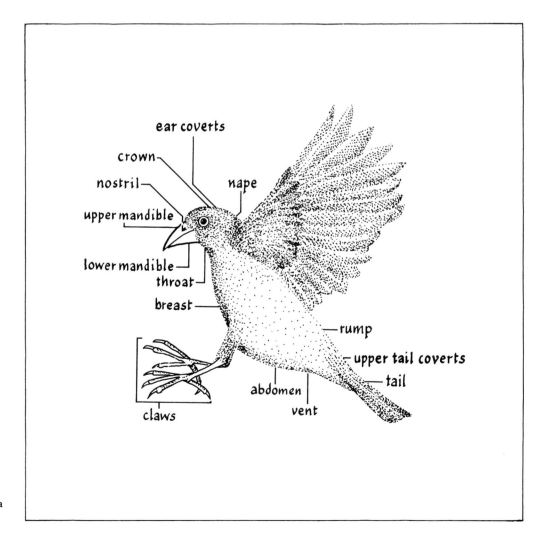

The main features of a bird's body

RED AVADAVAT
Amandava amandava
Origin: India, Sri Lanka and Malaysia

● ○

This bird is an excellent choice for a novice fancier. It is attractive in colouring and pleasantly disposed to other birds in a mixed collection. It is willing to breed in an aviary, away from aggressive birds. The cock bird's song is delightful although of short duration.

Description:
Size: 10 to 13 cm (4 to 5 in)
COCK:
Beak: red. Wings: dark brown. Sides and breast spotted with white. Body: bright red. Tail: black. Legs: brown. This is the only waxbill that has an eclipse plumage outside the breeding season, when the brightly coloured cock bird moults to resemble the drab coloured hen.
HEN:
Beak: red. Body: dark brown with beige on abdomen. Wings: spotted with white. Upper tail coverts: red. Black stripe on ear coverts. Legs: brown. (Immature cocks look like hens.)

Diet: (Seedeater)
Mixed millets and spray millet are enjoyed. Plain canary seed should be provided in a separate container. Green-

A pair of Red Avadavats

food and seeding grasses are also relished, and grit and cuttlefish bone must be available.

This waxbill winters successfully outside without heat, needing only a frost-proof shelter. It survives healthily for many years outside in a planted aviary where the plumage retains its beautiful red colour better than if housed inside.

Breeding:

The cock bird performs a prancing courtship dance displaying his spread tail with great pride.

This bird makes use of a wicker basket or builds its own nest in dense shrubbery. It does not like to breed in enclosed boxes as much as other small finches. The hen lays between four and six eggs which she incubates, without assistance from the cock, for around 12 days. When the chicks hatch, the parents should be given small live insects, sprouted seeds and seeding grasses to feed them with.

This species shows a strange preference for using black chicken feathers to line the nest, arranged in the form of a screen. The provision of such feathers by a thoughtful owner encourages nesting, as do Box bushes. This bird builds its hanging, pouch-shaped nest inside the bush sometimes with two entrances.

BENGALESE ● ○ ■
Lonchura domestica
Origin: China and Japan

A domesticated species developed originally by the Japanese as a fertile hybrid, by using members of the genus Lonchura (members of the mannikin family) which they imported from China. This species is very easy to manage and thus, an ideal bird for the novice. It is keen to reproduce and is very useful as a foster parent for Australian finches.

Description:

Size: 13 cm (5 in)
Several different colour forms exist including white, chocolate and white, chestnut and white, fawn and crested.

COCK:
Beak: Two-tone colour. Body: white with either chocolate, chestnut or fawn patterning. Markings vary greatly. Wings and tail usually show plenty of white. Legs: dark or pale.

HEN:
As cock. Both birds are stocky with a heavy beak.

The sex of Bengalese cannot be determined by physical appearance, only by behaviour. The cock bird puffs himself up

A group of fawn and white Bengalese

A Bicheno, the smallest
Australian finch

to resemble a small balloon while singing
his pleasant song. It is recommended that
several true pairs of Bengalese are kept for
fostering orphans in a mixed collection of
finches.

Bengalese love to bathe and should be
provided with suitable facilities. This
species may need to have its nails clipped,
as they tend to grow too long.

Diet: (Seedeater)

Plain canary seed and mixed millets form
the basic diet. Millet sprays and sprouted
seed may be given as a treat. Grit and cuttlefish bone must always be available.

Breeding:

Bengalese commence breeding as early as
eight months of age. Nest boxes should be
provided with a rather small entrance hole,
much preferred by this species. A rather
untidy nest is made inside the box and the
birds like to be well hidden while
incubating. Six to eight eggs are normally

laid and both parents sit side by side in the
nest during the incubation period of 14
days. The young are carefully fed by both
parents for about 21 days. When rearing
their young, Bengalese should be provided
with egg food, soaked bread, mealworms
and some greenfood. A few drops of cod
liver oil may be added to the rearing food
for young chicks. Youngsters should be
given soaked seed for the early weeks of
their life. Once independent, Bengalese
may be kept on dry seed outside the
breeding season.

BICHENO ●○■
Stizoptera bicheonovii
Origin: Australia

The smallest Australian finch, suitable for
a mixed collection of similar sized birds as
it is good tempered and docile However, it
defends its nest site vigorously if threatened.

This is a lively, amusing bird. It is hardy

and although it prefers a temperature of 15°C (60°F), it will survive in reasonable health at lower temperatures providing accommodation is dry and frost-proof.

Description:
Size: 10 cm (4 in)

COCK:

Beak: silver. Body: grey and white with black bands around chest and breast. Wings: dark blackish-grey flecked with white. Legs: grey.

HEN:

Almost identical, but on some birds, breast appears whiter than the cock's. If mating these birds, it is best to acquire several and let them pair themselves.

Diet: (Seedeater)
Mixed millets and small plain canary seed form the basic diet. Maw and the black niger seed are two useful small seed varieties which may also be given. Grit and cuttlefish bone must always be available.

Breeding:
The Bicheno nests in a box, in an old disused nest or in a bush. It does not use much material but lines the nest with soft materials, such as feathers and wool.

The courtship dance of the cock is rather basic and consists of his hopping towards the hen, turning in 180-degree circles with each hop. Part of the courtship ritual is wiping the beak on the perch.

Four to six white eggs are laid and both parents share in the incubation, never leaving the nest unattended. The sitting bird does not vacate the nest until the relief partner has entered. The cock bird is heard to sing at this time, normally a rare occurrence except in immature cock birds. The chicks hatch in 12 days and are fed by both parents. They emerge from the nest at 19 to 25 days. Soaked and sprouted seed should be fed to breeding pairs and propietary brand canary rearing food may be purchased and can be mixed with hard boiled egg. Chopped mealworms two or three per bird) are a useful aid.

It is an interesting sight to see a Bicheno Finch being fed by its parent on a perch. The chick raises one wing as if protecting its brothers and sisters alongside it from the parent bird. Young chicks are grey on upperparts and white below. There is no transverse band. The young birds may

safely be left with their tolerant parents while a second brood is reared. They often help in the feeding of the new chicks. Young birds commence their moult at seven weeks of age and usually complete this by 16 weeks of age.

Bichenos like to roost in boxes all year round so these should be available. It is advisable in this case to segregate the sexes outside the breeding season. Plastic split rings may be used to identify the pairs for future reference.

This friendly and lively bird often forms close friendships with others and this may account for the fact that it has often hybridised with other kinds of finch.

BUDGERIGAR □ ◀
Melopsittacus undulatus
Origin: Australia

The budgerigar is one of the oldest established popular pet birds. It is very easy to manage, eager to breed, good natured and companionable. It is particularly well liked by children. It may be kept in an outdoor flight all year round, providing there is adequate shelter from cold winds.

Description:
Size: 20 cm (8 in)

COCK:

There are many different coloured budgerigars, including blue, lilac, yellow, white and variegated. The original colour of this bird is green. All colours bear a mask with black throat spots. The cock has a blue cere.

HEN:

May be distinguished by the brown cere. There is a set standard of deportment, body size and shape for those being exhibited. Variations in the ideal standard have developed over the years, and differ according to locality. Consult your local bird club for information.

Diet: (Seedeater)
Standard budgerigar mix forms the basic diet and may be purchased very easily. Millet sprays and greenfood are enjoyed. When preparing birds for breeding, add cod liver oil to seed to help prevent egg binding. Grit and cuttlefish bone must always be available.

Opposite page: a pair of Budgerigars

Breeding:

When breeding it is a good idea to keep only one or two colours of budgerigar to avoid indiscriminate pairing. While peaceful with other birds, they are intolerant with others of their own kind, particularly if insufficient nest sites are available. Never keep an extra cock bird in the quarters, though an extra hen is not a problem, for she becomes a second wife. Once breeding commences, do not add further birds to the aviary or they may be attacked.

A budgerigar should not be allowed to breed before it is eight months of age, and then no more than three broods per year should be permitted, or the hen becomes exhausted and produces inferior quality chicks.

Nest boxes should be hung in the shelter and flight, but must be protected from heavy rain. This bird tends to sit in the opening to the nest box thus preventing air from reaching its young, so it is a good idea to make ventilation holes in the box.

During the breeding season, a pair should be given mixed millets, canary seed, sunflower seed, sweetcorn (maize), chickweed and lettuce. Willow and apple twigs are enjoyed.

A Black-Crested Bulbul

More eggs are usually laid in the second clutch than in the first. The maximum number of eggs in a clutch is eight. Incubation takes about 18 days, and the cock bird feeds his hen on the nest. The young fledge after about a month and sometimes new eggs are found amongst the fledglings as they are about to leave the nest.

BLACK-CRESTED BULBUL ◆
Pycnonotus melanicterus
Origin: India and Sri Lanka

An ideal softbill for the beginner, the Black-Crested Bulbul is very hardy and easy to manage. A single bird can be kept in a mixed aviary with birds of similar size and temperament. It lives happily with mynahs, Pekin Robins, starlings or seed-eaters such as whydahs and large weaver species. This lively bulbul becomes very tame with its owner.

Description:
Size: 20 cm (8 in)
COCK:
Head, crest and throat: black. Breast and upper parts: olive green, fading to dull yellowish-olive on belly and around the vent. Rather striking yellow eye. Beak and legs: black.
HEN:
As cock.

Diet: (Softbill)
Proprietary brand insectile mix and fruit including apples, oranges and particularly pears and chopped grapes, are favourites. It loves berries and should have a daily allowance of livefood. Six mealworms per bird can be given each day. The insectile mix should be coarse grained rather than fine.

Breeding:
In order to breed this charming bird it is necessary to segregate a pair in a flight on their own. It builds a rather messy cup-shaped nest in bushy vegetation, but has been known to utilise boxes or baskets in captivity. A thickly planted area must be provided or it does not attempt to build a nest.

Two to three eggs are laid and both cock and hen share in the building of the nest and in the incubation of the eggs and

rearing the young. Incubation normally lasts about 14 to 16 days and the chicks mature quickly when hatched and are ready to leave the nest after two weeks.

Successful rearing of chicks depends on the provision of plenty of livefood, mealworms, maggots, woodlice, small smooth backed caterpillars, grasshoppers and small locusts, which are ideal.

Two broods per season are normal. The chicks should be removed from the parents as soon as they are able to feed themselves, or they may be attacked by their elders who soon become intolerant of their young.

CANARY ◼ ◇
Serinus canaria
Origin: Canary Islands

This popular song bird can be obtained in a great variety of forms and colours. The wild canary was a green colour. It is possible to breed birds of all types in many different colours. The feather texture also varies in the different colours. Currently one of the most popular varieties is the one known as the Border Fancy. This is described below.

Description:
Size: **14 cm** (5½ in)
COCK:
Available in a wide range of colours including yellow (buff), white, green, cinnamon. Beak: small and conical. Eyes: bold and dark. Chest: well rounded, tapering towards underparts. The stance of a good show specimen should give an angle of 60 degrees when perching. It should appear alert and lively.
HEN:
Similar, but she is usually lighter or duller in colour. The most reliable indication as to sex is the song of the cock bird. The hen merely chirps.

Diet: (Seedeater)
Proprietary brand canary mixture is easily purchased, containing a blended mix of all the necessary seeds. Some groats and niger seed may be added in cold weather.

61

Greenfood should be supplied on a regular basis. Grit and cuttlefish bone must always be available.

Breeding:

It is most important to make sure that cock and hen are *both* in breeding condition. If either partner is not ready, any attempt at mating will prove unsuccessful.

Canary nest pans, easily purchased from pet stores, should be provided. These are lined with felt nest liners or other soft material. Canaries also nest in square wooden nest boxes fitted with perforated zinc bases. In very warm weather, zinc based boxes allow plenty of cool air to circulate for the comfort of sitting birds.

Four to five eggs are laid on consecutive days. The eggs should be removed one by one and stored and marked in number order in a felt lined box. Artificial eggs, purchased from pet stores, must be placed under the hen until the evening of the fourth day, when they should be removed and the real eggs replaced so she may start incubation. The incubation period is 13 to 14 days. This is the normal practice in canary breeding.

If the hen is reluctant to bathe, the eggs should be moisted with warm water while she is off the nest feeding. Proprietary brand canary rearing food is available from pet stores and wholemeal bread and milk may be offered. Chickweed is eagerly consumed by breeding birds.

Canary chicks grow very quickly so the rearing food must be regularly increased in quantity. Within 16 to 20 days, chicks are ready to leave the nest. They are dependent on their parents for food for a further ten days. By the time the brood is fully independent, the hen is usually ready to lay again.

Canaries are often cross-bred with certain British finches to produce attractive hybrids known as "mules".

GREEN CARDINAL ◀ ◇
Gubernatrix Cristata
Origin: Brazil and Argentina

This is an interesting variety of cardinal and a single bird can be kept quite safely in a mixed collection. However, pairs need to be watched to make sure there is no fighting. A suitable group of companions

A Green Cardinal

for this species should include such types as whydahs, weavers and Java Sparrows. Although less colourful than the Red-Crested and Pope Cardinal, the Green Cardinal is often more eager to breed.

Description:
Size: 20 cm (8 in)
COCK:
Body: olive green with black markings. Cheeks and throat: yellow. Crest and throat patch: black. Stomach: greenish-yellow. Beak: grey. Legs: dark grey.
HEN:
Body: grey-green and greyish-white. May be sexed fairly easily.

Diet: (Seedeater)
Plain canary seed, mixed millets, sunflower seed and hemp form the basic diet. Some livefood, fruit tree twigs, grit and cuttlefish bone should be provided.

This hardy species can tolerate low temperatures, but not damp conditions. It is easy to keep in a medium sized aviary with a dry, damp-proof shelter for cold weather.

Breeding:
Pairs construct a nest in a fairly dense bush or shrub. An open-fronted nest box, a basket or a cup-shaped receptacle should be provided to encourage breeding. Plenty of livefood should be given including small, smooth caterpillars, woodlice, spiders, fresh ants' eggs, wasp grubs and a few mealworms and maggots.

Three to four eggs form a normal clutch although as many as six are sometimes laid. Chicks fledge after four weeks and are normally independent in a further two weeks. Sprouted seeds and seeding grass heads should be fed to the chicks. Remove the young from their parents as soon as they are seen to be eating well on their own.

POPE CARDINAL ◀ ◇
Paroaria dominicana
Origin: Brazil

This lively, attractive song bird resembles the Red-Crested Cardinal, but is better tempered, smaller and has no crest. It has a

A Pope Cardinal (top centre) amongst Red-Crested Cardinals

very melodious voice. It is not aggressive with similar sized birds, but a pair are shy of breeding in a mixed collection.

Description:
Size: 18 cm (7 in)
COCK:
Head and throat: bright red. Stomach: white, fading to grey. Back, wings and tail: dark grey. Beak: cream. Legs: dark grey.
HEN:
Identical, so it is ifficult to select a true pair.

Diet: (Seedeater)
Plain canary seed, mixed millets and a little sunflower seed form the basic diet. If available, hemp seed is enjoyed. Some birds enjoy a little fruit. Greenfood and livefood should be given to breeding pairs and an occasional maggot or mealworm is appreciated out of the breeding season. Grit and cuttlefish bone must always be available.

This bird needs a large aviary with plenty of cover. It is hardy, but should be encouraged to use a shelter in cold weather as it has a habit of roosting outside. If not keen to use a shelter, try to provide some outside cover near the favourite perching and roosting spot.

Breeding:
As pairs are nervous and shy, it is better to remove the birds to a separate quiet area for breeding. The hen chooses her mate carefully, so it is advisable to purchase several birds and allow natural pairing. Its nesting habits are much the same as the Red-Crested Cardinal.

An artificial nest site should be provided at shoulder level. An untidy nest is constructed from grasses and heathers, if available. A willow basket often proves a popular nesting site as do thick bushes.

Four to six eggs are laid and both parents take turns in incubation and feeding. Plenty of livefood should be provided, together with hard boiled egg and fresh ants' eggs. When the young fledge, they should continue to be fed the same diet.

RED-CRESTED CARDINAL ◀ ◇
Paroaria cucullata
Origin: South America

A striking bird that immediately catches the eye. It is bold and confident, good for exhibiting and tames quite easily. It may be kept with such birds as weavers, whydahs, Cut-Throat Finches, Java Sparrows or with a Group 3 softbill (see p. 52).

A Red-Crested Cardinal

Description:
Size: 20 cm (8 in)
COCK:
Crest: red. Body: grey and white. Eyes: black. Legs: black. Tail: black.
HEN:
Similar, but slightly smaller and slimmer. The only sure indication of sex is the cock's rather attractive song during the breeding season.

Diet: (Seedeater)
Plain canary seed and mixed millets form the basic diet. It also enjoys a little plain sunflower seed. Insectile mix, mealworms and fresh ants' eggs are eagerly devoured. Grit and cuttlefish bone must always be available.

This bird lives happily in most temperatures, but may often be seen basking in a patch of sunlight on the ground. A frost-proof shelter should be provided for cold weather.

Breeding:
Nesting takes place in untidily built nests about knee high from the ground. These are built in thick bushes or hedges. Heather and grass blades are often used for nesting material. Willow or wicker baskets can be used as a base.

Both parents share in incubation of the eggs and rearing of the young. Four to six eggs form a normal clutch. Hard boiled egg may be added to the normal diet for rearing. This species appreciates plentiful livefood when breeding and will eat small smooth backed caterpillars, maggots, locusts and woodlice. Spiders are often enjoyed.

When first leaving the nest the chicks have ginger coloured crests and are easily recognised from their parents. The young birds are sometimes fed at ground level after fledging and the chicks flutter their tail feathers while wittering for attention. The Red-Crested Cardinal is usually a very protective parent.

Once mature, this species has a tendency to put on weight. So provide a large flight to prevent it becoming lazy and taking insufficient exercise.

CHESTNUT-BREASTED FINCH ○ ■
Lonchura castaneothorax
Origin: Australia

This Australian finch is beautifully marked and its plumage is glossy and smooth. It is easy to keep and quite hardy. This species

A Chestnut-Breasted Finch

does well in a medium-sized aviary and mixes amicably with other seedeaters of similar size.

Description:
Size: 10 to 13 cm (4 to 5 in)
COCK:
Head: black. Chest: chestnut with a black band above stomach. Stomach: creamy-beige. Shoulders, wings and tail: dark chestnut. Legs: grey. Beak: blue-grey. Eyes: black.
HEN:
Identical, but the cock sings and the hen does not.

Diet: (Seedeater)
Plain canary seed, mixed millets, green-food and a little livefood form the basic diet. Grit and cuttlefish bone must always be available. This species can be lethargic and has a tendency to put on weight, so do not overfeed.

Breeding:
This species makes a very attentive parent, but may attempt to breed at a very early age and should not be allowed to do so. Chestnut-Breasted cock birds also show a preference for Bengalese hens if housed with this species, so do not mix them if you wish to avoid cross-breeding. Nest boxes should be placed in the aviary and try to provide some grass clippings, so that the pair may fill their chosen site. The nest is filled to overflowing and the eggs laid precariously on top.

Five or six large white eggs form the normal clutch. After three or four eggs are laid, both parents share incubation which takes 13 days.

Provide hard boiled egg, insectile mix and soaked and sprouted seed for the parents to rear their brood. The young chicks become rather nervous as they grow and great care should be taken when they are about 18 to 22 days old, as they sometimes leave the nest too early if alarmed, which may prove fatal.

The Chestnut-Breasted Finch does not roost in next boxes, so ensure that they are in the shelter by nightfall in colder weather. This species has a tendency to overgrown claws, so try to clip them at least three or four times a year.

COCKATIEL
Nymphicus hollandicus
Origin: Australia

The Cockatiel is an interesting parrotlike species for the novice bird keeper. It is easy to house, feed and breed. It is also a very gentle bird and may be kept with other compatible species including small finches. When breeding, however, it should have its own accommodation, preferably with a large wooden nest box hung in a quiet corner of the flight. The Cockatiel needs a long flight since it is a strong flyer and needs ample space to exercise its wings. It may share breeding quarters with budgerigars.

Description:
Size: 33 cm (13 in)
COCK:
Several different colour forms exist, including a Lutino variety. The familiar grey Cockatiel is easily recognised by its attractive crest.
Upperparts: dark grey. Under surfaces: light grey and yellowish-buff. Front of head and crest, cheeks and throat: bright yellow. Ear coverts: orange. A striking white band runs down the centre of the wings. Beak and legs: dark grey.

A Lutino Cockatiel at the nest box

HEN:
Similar, but underside of tail is barred with yellow and grey. The yellow on the face is duller than on the cock.

Diet: (Seedeater)
Plain canary seed, mixed millets and a little sunflower and hemp seed form the basic diet. Fresh greenfood and fruit such as apple and pear, should be provided. Plentiful supplies of grit and cuttlefish are essential.

Breeding:
The Cockatiel is a prolific breeder and goes to nest three times in a season. Six or more eggs may be laid in one clutch. Breeding pairs should be fed on soaked seed and bread and milk to produce top quality chicks. Both parents share in the incubation of the eggs which takes from 19 to 21 days. The young fledge between four and five weeks.

CUT-THROAT FINCH ◀
Amadina fasciata
Origin: Africa

This extremely hardy finch lives healthily in an outside aviary for many years. It is sometimes inclined to be aggressive and should only be kept with weavers, whydahs, Java Sparrows, cardinals and other large sized birds. It is easy to manage and is a sensible choice for the novice fancier.

Description:
Size: 13 cm (5 in)
COCK:
Body: Beige-brown dappled with dark greyish-black, looking like scales. Beak: grey. Legs: dull pink. Throat: scarlet.
HEN:
Similar, but lacks scarlet throat patch, therefore easy to sex.

A pair of hardy Cut-Throat Finches

Diet: (Seedeater)

Mixed millets, plain canary seed and seeding grasses form the basic diet. Greenfood is appreciated. Grit and cuttlefish bone must always be available.

This bird may be kept out of doors all year round, needing only a dry, frost-proof shelter in cold weather.

Breeding:

In display, the Cut-Throat cock sings a quiet little song, ruffling his throat feathers as he sings. A nest is built from grasses, roots, hairs or any available material, preferably inside a nest box. It is normally lined with feathers. The hen lays four to six eggs which both parents take turns to incubate. The young are normally hatched after 12 days incubation. Rearing food should consist of soaked and sprouted seeds, soaked stale bread, a few mealworms and fresh ants' eggs. Nest inspection is resented while the parents are sitting, so avoid disturbance to prevent desertion of the nest.

During the breeding season it is a good idea to mix cod liver oil with the birds' seed, since this helps prevent egg binding to which Cut-Throat hens are often prone. In cold weather, the same measure may be taken to ensure health and vitality. Another aid during the breeding season is sponge cake soaked in honey and a little fine grade insectile mix.

DIAMOND SPARROW ○ ■
Staganopleura guttata
Origin: Australia

The colourful Diamond Sparrow is one of the most easily bred Australian finches. A pair in a mixed collection may be well behaved towards the other inhabitants or very aggressive, for individual temperaments vary greatly in this species.

Assuming a pleasant natured pair, they should go to nest happily without inconveniencing other birds.

Description:
Size: 13 cm (5 in)
COCK:
Head: grey. Throat: white. Back: grey. Sides: black dotted with white spots. Black band on chest. Rump: scarlet. Belly: white. Legs: grey. Beak: red.

HEN:
Similar in appearance, but the hen has a paler red rim around the eye than the cock. The cock bird's song is a short rasping note and the hen merely chirps.

Diet: (Seedeater)
Small plain canary seed and mixed millets form the basic diet, with some greenfood. Grit and cuttlefish bone must always be available.

Since this bird spends much of its time on the ground, it should be shut inside the shelter during very heavy rain to prevent chills.

Breeding:
The display of the cock is the best indication of the bird's sex. He approaches the hen holding a long grass stalk in his beak whilst fully stretching his neck upwards, then lowers his head until his beak almost touches his chest and hops closer to the hen in an ungainly fashion. Although the hen usually looks bored with his antics, this signifies that she has accepted him as her mate. If the hen is not interested she flies off.

Diamond Sparrows nest in half-fronted nest boxes in which they construct their own domed nest. Pairs re-arrange the nest several times until it is considered perfect. The hen often plucks white feathers from her own breast to line the nest.

Six eggs form the maximum clutch and both parents incubate the eggs. On changing over, the sitters call out to each other with a strange snore-like noise whereupon they swop over. They commence sitting as soon as the first egg is laid.

Offer as much livefood as possible during breeding, including fresh ants' eggs and boiled mealworms, finely chopped with a plentiful supply of grit.

The chicks are easily reared and leave the nest in 22 to 24 days. In the first few weeks they return to the nest to be fed and to sleep. Nest inspection is not usually resented by Diamond Sparrows. Once independent the young should be removed from their intolerant parents unless the aviary is very large. The young moult out between seven and 13 weeks of age.

Diamond Sparrows who go to nest too young should have their chicks removed for fostering by Bengalese. Do not place more than three young chicks with one pair

Opposite: a Diamond Sparrow

of Bengalese, since Diamond Sparrow chicks eat particularly large quantities of food.

Diamond Sparrows have a habit of plucking each other and also sometimes their neighbours, so should be watched for this bad habit. The cause is not known.

Once the initial difficulty of obtaining a true pair is overcome, breeding results should be good.

DIAMOND DOVE ○ ■
Geopelia c. cuneata
Origin: Australia

The Diamond Dove is particularly suitable for keeping with seedeaters in a mixed collection. It is a useful ground bird which eats seed on the floor that might otherwise go to waste. It is one of the smallest of the dove family, but is intolerant of other doves of any type, so only one pair is recommended per aviary. Although this bird spends most of its time in the aviary at ground level, it may also be seen perching in bushes off the ground.

Description:
Size: 18 cm (7½ in)

COCK:
Head, neck and breast: pale silver-grey. Nape and back: pale brown. Wing coverts: dark grey with a round white spot near each feather tip. Tail: central feathers dark grey with black towards the tips. Eyes: orange-yellow or red. Eye ring: bright coral red. Beak: olive brown. Legs and feet: red.

HEN:
Similar, but slightly smaller with a thinner head. During the breeding season the hen's eye ring is a paler red. At other times, the clearest indication as to sex is the cock's fascinating display with spread tail.

Right: a Diamond Dove

Opposite: a pair of Laughing Doves

Diet: (Seedeater)
Mixed millets, plain canary seed and maw seed in small quantities form the basic diet. It also enjoys insectile mixture, an occasional mealworm, ants' eggs and greenfood, particularly chopped young cabbage leaves. Grit must always be available.

The Diamond Dove can be housed outside all year round, but needs a dry place to roost. As this species may take fright after dark and injure itself or others, it needs an enclosed shelter.

Breeding:
The Diamond Dove prefers nest pans or shallow boxes for nesting. These are filled with twigs, coarse grass and moss. The cock displays eagerly to the hen by dancing around her, while fanning out his tail and beating his wings on the ground.

Two eggs are the normal clutch and from these a cock and hen emerge. Both parents take turns on sitting on the eggs for the 13-day incubation period. Rearing food should consist of sprouted seeds and soaked bread. Once the chicks are independent they should be removed from their parents otherwise they are chased away when a new round of eggs is laid.

Brothers and sisters may be paired together when adult. This does no harm but they should not be paired often or inbreeding may result, impairing the quality of the young.

LAUGHING DOVE □ ◄
Streptopelia senegalensis
Origin: Africa

A very suitable species for inclusion in a mixed collection, as it is a very tame dove, which is far more lively than most other types. It does not, however, agree with its own kind, so only one pair should be included in an aviary.

Description:
Size: 25 cm (10 in)

COCK:
Head, throat and chest: reddish-brown. Collar: black. Upperparts: reddish-brown, merging into grey. Stomach: white. Chin: white. Eyes: brown. Eyelids: red. Beak: black. Legs: red.

HEN:
Grey all over.

Diet: (Seedeater)
Mixed millets, oats and hemp, if available, form the basic diet. Occasional greenfood and a few insects are enjoyed, but these are not essential.

Breeding:
Pairs frequently choose a conifer as a nest site and build a rather messy nest from twigs and straw. Try to provide a wire mesh base to start off the construction for these rather inept nest builders.

Two eggs are laid and both cock and hen share in the incubation which takes 13 days. The cock feeds the hen at this time. When the two chicks emerge they usually prove to be a cock and a hen. They are almost totally independent in a further 12 days and should then be taken away from their parents, as a new round is started immediately.

This species can produce up to five or six broods in one season, but more than five should not be allowed, or the hen may become exhausted and produce inferior chicks.

An Asian Fairy Bluebird. Note the small feet in relation to its size.

ASIAN FAIRY BLUEBIRD △
Irene puella
Origin: India, Thailand and South East Asia

An easy-to-manage, fruit biased omnivorous softbill, which, once acclimatised, is hardy enough to winter outside needing only a frost-proof shelter. It has a melodious call and makes a very delightful sight flying in the aviary with its bright blue colour and engaging ways. It has very small, delicate feet in relation to its body size and its toes must be protected from frost bite.

This species is able to fly very strongly and needs a spacious aviary. If unable to obtain a pair, one sole cock bird lives quite happily on its own among similar types in a mixed collection, and becomes very tame with its owner.

Description:
Size: 25 cm (10 in)
COCK:
Mantle: blue. Back and area down to base of tail: blue. Other areas: shiny, velvet black. Eyes: red with black pupils.
HEN:
Very similar, but a far more dusky blue. Both cock and hen birds are heavy bodied.

Diet: (Softbill)
Bananas, pears, oranges, soft fruit, currants, sultanas and raisins form the basic diet. Raw minced meat should be given and honey and water mixture poured over sponge cake or stale bread makes a welcome addition to the diet. Livefood, such as mealworms and well cleaned maggots, is neccessary. Hard boiled egg mash is enjoyed. All these ingredients can be mixed together in one dish in the following percentages: 65% fruit, 10% raw minced meat; 10% sponge cake or bread; 10% coarse grade insectile mix and 5% live food. Nectar mix made from proprietary brand nectar powder and honey and water, or sugar and water, may be given in a dish on its own.

Breeding:
The Asian Fairy Bluebird is not too difficult to persuade to breed. It is sometimes difficult to obtain pairs of this attractive species, but zoos and bird

gardens occasionally part with surplus stock to keen fanciers.

Pairs use a shallow cup-shaped nesting basket if provided, lined with fine grasses and moss. If left to build their own, they make untidy looking nests in dense bushes, quite high up. Just two small olive grey eggs with brown speckles are laid. Plenty of livefood is necessary for chick rearing.

The Asian Fairy Bluebird is fairly docile in a mixed collection of birds of similar size. During the breeding season, however, cock birds can be bad tempered towards their own kind, if several pairs are kept in the same aviary.

A Vinaceous Fire Finch

VINACEOUS FIRE FINCH ●○
Lagonosticta larvata vinacea
Origin: West Africa

A very peaceful waxbill, similar to the African Fire Finch, that readily agrees with others and is very attractive. This species may be housed in quite a small aviary with other small seedeaters, but must have a little extra warmth in cold weather.

Description:
Size: 10 to 13 cm (4 to 5 in)
COCK:
Head: dark grey. Black stripe above beak, across eyes and cheeks. Throat: black. Back, breast and stomach: wine red. White spots on sides of breast. Underparts: black. Tail: dark red. Wings: brown. Beak: grey.
HEN:
Body: greyish-brown with a red cast. Stomach: pinkish-beige. Head: light grey.

Diet: (Seedeater)
The basic diet consists of mixed millets, spray millet, soaked and sprouted seed, chopped mealworms and insects as available. Grit and cuttlefish bone must always be available.

Breeding:
Pairs go to to nest quite readily, building a round nest from available materials, such as soft grasses and mosses.

Three to five eggs are laid which hatch in 11 days. Both parents share in the incubation. Try to provide fresh ants' eggs, chopped mealworms and mashed egg yolk. Dried ants' eggs should be soaked in warm water, prior to feeding.

A Golden-Fronted Fruitsucker

GOLDEN-FRONTED △
FRUITSUCKER
Chloropsis aurifrons
Origin: Himalayas and Burma

One of the most colourful softbills available, this supremely graceful bird also has a delightful, melodious song. It soon becomes tame with its owner and eagerly takes a daily mealworm from the hand. It makes an excellent show bird and is often a very clever mimic of other birds. It is best kept with birds of similar size such as large tanagers, jays, starlings and Pekin Robins in a well sized, planted aviary.

Description:
Size: 20 cm (8 in)
COCK:
Body: bright green, shoulder patch of turquoise-blue. Head: gold on crown. Side of head and neck: black. Cheeks sport a blue band. Underside: light green. Tail: green and navy blue. Beak: black. Legs: dark grey.
HEN:
Similar, but slightly duller colours.

Diet: (Softbill)

Most fruits, including pear, orange, banana and grapes, form the basic diet. Try scooping out an orange and refilling the centre with coarse grade insectile mix and orange pieces, and watch this bird delight in dipping into it. It loves to suck the juice from a halved orange. Raisins, chopped dates, currants and sultanas are all eagerly taken. Mealworms and well cleaned maggots are among the most suitable live food for this species and other insects should be provided as available. Egg yolk and minced meat are very suitable additions to the diet. Food should be placed on a pedestal high off the ground to keep it clean as this bird often treads around in dishes. The Golden-Fronted Fruitsucker often carries a morsel of food to a favourite perching spot and daintily consumes it.

This bird is aggressive with its own kind so only a sole bird or a known true pair should be kept. It does not cause problems when housed with other species.

Breeding:

A pair will go to nest more readily if housed alone. When nesting, pairs build cup-shaped nests high up in trees or shrubs as they need great privacy. Few eggs are laid, probably two at a maximum. Breeding birds should be fed plenty of soft fruits, insects and sponge cake soaked in honey and water.

This species loves to bathe and should, if possible, have a small pool or bird bath. It enjoys flicking raindrops from wet foliage on to its plumage.

All types of fruitsucker should be carefully acclimatised. Although it becomes quite hardy in time, it is advisable to house the Golden-Fronted Fruitsucker in a conservatory in winter, as it cannot tolerate frost.

GOLDFINCH ■ ◇

Carduelis carduelis
Origin: United Kingdom/Europe

The Goldfinch has been kept and bred by numerous fanciers in Great Britain for centuries, being particularly popular in the Victorian era. It is noted for its soft, sweet song and is always tame and friendly. It thrives well when housed with canaries in a mixed collection.

Description:

Size: 13 cm (5 in)

COCK:

Eyes: light brown. Beak: light cream, blackish on tip. Mask: red edged with white, the red often fades in aviary specimens. Crown, side of neck and wings: black. Wings also show bands of yellow and white spots at tips of flights. Back: brown. Upper tail coverts: buff. Underparts: white, tinged with brown. Tail: black with white edges. Feet and legs: light brown.

HEN:

Very similar, but the mask is slightly smaller and a duller red. Sometimes a little difficult to sex by appearance.

Diet: (Seedeater)

Niger is the most favoured seed. Canary mixture, oats, groats and some hulled sunflower seed should also be given. It also enjoys hemp, but sunflower seed is a ready substitute in countries where hemp is illegal. Greenfood is enjoyed and thistles are relished by this species. Grit and cuttlefish bone must always be provided.

Breeding:

This species is usually rather keen to breed. Pairs make neat, compact, small nests with dried grasses, hair, wool and feathers. Four to six eggs are laid and the incubation period is 13 days. The hen sits alone but parents share in feeding the young. Two nests per year can be expected from pairs.

Cock Goldfinches also mate readily with other British finches and canaries producing attractive hybrids and colourful mules.

A Goldfinch

GOULDIAN FINCH ○ ■

Chloebia gouldiae, sometimes known as
Poephila gouldiae
Origin: Northern Australia

A particularly colourful, beautiful species
of finch which exhibits well and is
peaceful with other species. It can be
housed outdoors during the summer
months, but is best housed indoors unless
kept in a warm climate. A mean
temperature of 15°C (60°F) should be
maintained for best results. Although it
can be acclimatised to live without heat, it
must always be protected from draughts. It
is often lethargic so should be encouraged
to take exercise by placing perches some
distance apart.

Description:

Size: 13 cm (5 in)
Three colour forms exist: the Red-Headed
Gouldian, Black-Headed Gouldian and
Yellow-Headed Gouldian. There is also a
White-Breasted mutation. Basic colours of
the description are the same, as only the
head colour differs.
Example: Red-Headed Gouldian.
COCK:
Lower neck, mantle and wings: green.
Chest: bright purple. Lower breast and
stomach: saffron-yellow. Back of head and
rump: lilac. Face and head: red bordered
with black. Beak: cream. Legs: flesh
colour.
HEN:
Similar, but her chest is pale mauve. Other
colours are slightly duller. Adult birds are
easy to sex. Since Gouldians are reputed to
be difficult to keep alive, only fully
moulted out, adult specimens should be
purchased for breeding purposes.

Diet: (Seedeater)

Best quality mixed millets and small plain
canary seed from the basic diet. Proprietary brand foreign finch mix may be
purchased for this bird. Greenfood is
desirable, but is not always taken, and grit
and flaked cuttlefish bone are essential.
Granulated charcoal should also be provided, as it is enjoyed by this species. Many
fanciers prefer to feed soaked or sprouted
seed both during and outside the breeding
season. The Gouldian Finch should always
be given cold, boiled tap water to drink.

Breeding:

The courtship dance of the Gouldian Finch
is interesting to watch: he jumps up and
down on the perch trilling to his hen, who,
if agreeable, quivers her tail in response.

Open-fronted nest boxes with light
entrances, or globular wicker baskets, are
accepted as nest sites. Some pairs make fine
nests from long grasses inside the box
while others carry very little nesting
material inside.

Six eggs are normally laid and both
parents take turns in the incubation after
the third egg is laid. The young hatch in 16
days. The chicks have luminous mouth
spots to aid their parents in feeding inside
the dark of the nest. The hen sits in the nest
with the chicks while the cock guards the
entrance.

Parents rear their chicks with the aid of
brown bread soaked in milk and/or soaked
and sprouted seed.

Young Gouldians are coloured grey at
first and do not attain full mature colour
until almost a year of age. The juvenile
moult is particularly difficult for this
species. They should not be fed entirely on

**A Black-Headed
Gouldian cock with a
Red-Headed hen**

hard seed until they have gone through this moult.

The Gouldian should not be bred until fully adult (usually one year). Hens assume a black cast on the tip of the beak when ready for breeding. Pair bonding is very strong in this species. Separate pairs after breeding each year to give them a rest, but make sure the bird is re-united with the correct partner.

Sometimes this species is afflicted with a condition known as "twirling", which only seems to occur in Gouldians. The bird swings its head and neck around in a circular fashion. This can lead to premature death, so never use such a bird for breeding, as it seems to make this condition worse. The cause is not certain but may be attributed to in-breeding.

A Long-Tailed Grassfinch and (right) a Heck's Grassfinch

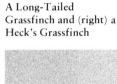

LONG-TAILED GRASSFINCH HECK'S GRASSFINCH
Poephila acuticauda
Origin: North West Australia

○ ■

The sleek and strikingly marked plumage of this lovely species makes it an eye catching attraction in any aviary. A steady specimen exhibits well. Two forms of this beautiful bird exist: the Long-Tailed Grassfinch, which sports a yellow beak and the Heck's Grassfinch, which has a coral beak. A bird with an orange beak is a cross of the two types.

This bird can be aggressive and is best kept with Diamond Sparrows and Zebra Finches.

Description:

Size: 18 cm (7 in)

COCK:

Head: silver-grey. Body and wings: fawnish-grey. Belly: paler fawn. Oval bib on throat and upper breast: black. Eye stripe: black. Thighs: black and white. Tail: black. Beak: yellow, coral or orange as explained above.

HEN:

Similar, but often has a smaller black bib. This bird is quite difficult to sex by appearance.

Diet: (Seedeater)

Plain canary seed and mixed millets form the basic diet. Millet sprays and seeding grasses are eagerly consumed. Greenfood is accepted by some of this species, but ignored by others. Grit and cuttlefish bone must always be available.

Although a fairly hardy species, it will fare better in cold weather if provided with some heat.

Breeding:

The cock bird displays by ruffling his bib whilst singing and performing a hopping jig before his intended mate.

This bird prefers to choose his own mate for breeding. Pair bonding between cocks and hens of this species is often for life and a compatible pair breed well, if conditions are suitable. A colony may be kept with the other recommended species so that there is plenty of choice for partner selection.

Breeding should not be contemplated before the pairs are a year old. As the hen is susceptible to egg binding even when mature, it is advisable to add cod liver oil to her seed once a week to prevent this problem.

Nest boxes and baskets should be placed in the aviary in medium height bushes giving a variety of choice.

A little privacy will encourage the birds to commence nesting preparations. Some cover should be provided with easy access. The nest will usually be lined with soft grasses, moss and feathers, so always provide plenty of nesting materials so that they will not fight over possession of favoured items.

Four to six white eggs are laid and incubation is shared by cock and hen with both parents roosting in the nest at night. The incubation period lasts 17 days. Nest inspection is not usually resented, but should be kept to a minimum. The young chicks are fed by their parents for 21 to 23 days.

During the rearing period, sprouted seed and extra millet sprays should be given. Bread and milk may also be fed, but take care not to allow the milk to sour. Soft rearing food mixed with hard boiled egg is eagerly taken, and some birds also enjoy chopped mealworms.

The young should be independent after a further month, and should be separated from their parents before further breeding. If birds are housed indoors, take the parents from the quarters and leave the young in the surroundings that they know. Some chicks have been known to refuse food and die after having been moved. It is better to move the parents than risk losing chicks. If housed out of doors, it is easier to partition off part of the flight while further broods are raised.

The parents should not be allowed to rear more than three broods a year otherwise they become exhausted and produce inferior chicks. As they attempt to breed all year round, cocks and hens should be separated after the third round. Split ring the progeny for future identification.

MASKED GRASSFINCH ○ ■

Poephila personata

Origin: Australia

This attractive grassfinch spends a great deal of time on the ground and is sometimes a little less hardy than other species of grassfinch. However, it thrives well if provided with suitable accommodation with protection against damp and cold. Although not aggressive, except in the breeding season, this bird has a tendency to disturb its aviary companions with frequent alarm calls for no particular reason. It is not a good bird to exhibit, since it sits on the cage floor too frequently.

Description:

Size: 13 cm (5 in)

COCK:

Body: cream-grey. Wings: beige. Tail, mask and upper thighs: black. Beak: yellow.

A group of Masked Grassfinches

Opposite: a Green Singing Finch

favoured dish until the young are independent. The juvenile moult commences when the chicks are nine weeks old. This species is sometimes rather aggressive during the breeding season, but is usually content to chase other birds away.

Masked Grassfinches have hybridised on many occasions with the Long-Tailed Grassfinch, Parson Finch, Zebra Finch, Bicheno, Cherry Finch and Chestnut-Breasted Finch.

If difficulties occur in rearing young Masked Grassfinches, Bengalese may be used as foster parents.

GREEN SINGING FINCH
Serinus mozambicus
Origin: Africa

This finch is a superb and popular, easy-to-manage song bird which is a distant relative of the canary. It is hardy and lives for a very long time, maybe attaining as much as 20 years of age under the right conditions.

Description:
Size: 10 to 13 cm (4 to 5 in)
COCK:
Head: grey. Neck and back: grey-green. Chin, throat and belly: yellow. Eyebrows: bright yellow with yellow patches on sides of chin. Wings and tail: black. There is a yellow edge to some of the wing feathers. Eyes: encircled with black stripe. Beak and legs: cream-grey.
HEN:
Similar, but easy to distinguish since she also sports a collar of black spots around her throat.

Diet: (Seedeater)
Plain canary seed and yellow millet form the staple diet. Spray millet is also much appreciated. Greenfood should be provided regularly and an occasional apple is enjoyed. Grit and cuttlefish bone must always be available.

This finch may be kept outside all year round but should have a dry, frost-proof shelter in which to roost.

This species does not require a large aviary since it is rarely seen to fly a great deal. If several pairs are kept, they usually all roost together at night on one single perch high in the shelter.

HEN:
Very similar but a little paler in colour with a slightly smaller mask. The hen's beak is also a paler yellow. Behaviour is a more reliable indication to the sex of the bird, but the cock must be watched carefully to spot the ruffling of his throat feathers and to hear his song.

Diet: (Seedeater)
Plain canary seed, mixed millet and finch tonic seed form the basic diet. Charcoal is a must for this species and should always be available, for without this breeding is not attempted. Grit and cuttlefish bone are also necessary.

Breeding:
Standard half-open nest boxes should be provided at low levels. If several pairs are kept, they should be allowed plenty of space between nesting sites. Once the hen has accepted a nest box, it is 21 days until the first egg is laid. Progress is far slower than that of other grassfinches. The nest building is a lengthy affair with both parents taking part in lining the nest with moss and feathers. The normal clutch is five eggs, with cock and hen sharing the incubation and rearing of the chicks.

Masked Grassfinches tend to rear their young on one solitary type of food. Some parents feed only sprouted seed, others only standard canary rearing food mixed with hard boiled egg or brown bread and milk. Some seek out livefood. Watch carefully to learn their preference and always provide larger amounts of the

Breeding:
Nests are built in shrubs or trees or an open-fronted nest box, if one is handy. The hen is responsible for constructing the nest and incubating the eggs. The incubation period is 13 days. While the hen is nest building and sitting, the cock perches nearby, singing frequently. During the incubation period, he sits close by the nest like a sentry on duty.

Breeding birds should be fed plenty of sprouted seed, grass seed and greenfood. They also benefit from finely chopped mealworms, egg and ants' eggs.

The young are independent 21 days after leaving the nest. The cock feeds the young for several weeks afterwards, but they should be removed from their parents

A Japanese Hawfinch

before further breeding takes place.

As well as breeding with its own kind, a cock may be mated with a small canary hen to produce an attractive mule.

Cock and hen Green Singing Finches show little interest in remaining together after the breeding season is over. The cock bird can be aggressive with its companions when breeding, but at other times is tolerant and peaceful, although there may be an occasional squabble with its mate out of breeding season.

Occasionally this species may be found to be suffering from sore eyes caused by wiping its face on a dirty perch. It appears short-sighted and may frequently have difficulty in finding the feed dish. Regular cleaning of perches prevents this problem.

JAPANESE HAWFINCH
Eophona personata
Origin: Japan

A seedeater with fairly simple requirements, this hardy species soon makes itself at home in a well planted aviary, although it may at first be shy. It enjoys roosting in trees of the evergreen variety. Despite the heavy beak, typical of the hawfinch family, it is peaceful and non-aggressive, but should be housed with birds of similar size, not smaller.

Its attractive, glossy plumage makes it a very handsome specimen and its immaculate appearance is maintained throughout the year, even when moulting. It is an excellent bird for exhibition.

Description:
Size: 20 cm (8 in)
COCK:
Head and throat: black. Neck: blue-grey. Belly: reddish-brown. Rump: white. Wings: black, barred with white. Tail: black. Beak: yellow with lilac patch at base. The tip of the beak is black. Legs: pink.
HEN:
Paler in colour. Head and throat: grey. Beak: yellow.

Diet: (Seedeater)
Plain canary seed, sunflower seed, a little hemp seed and some buckwheat form the basic diet. Regular supplies of greenfood and some livefood are much appreciated.

Grit and cuttlefish bone must always be available.

Breeding:
A pair of these birds may be encouraged to begin nesting in a wicker nest basket. The basket should be tied securely in a position with plenty of cover. Sometimes a pair builds a nest. A maximum of four eggs form the normal clutch and the hen sits alone for the 14-day incubation period. At this time, the pair should be supplied with plenty of livefood, such as, maggots, mealworms and small smooth caterpillars. Canary rearing food and extra greenfood are very beneficial.

YELLOW-COLLARED IXULUS ◆
Ixulus flavicollis
Origin: Himalayas

A small, drab coloured bird which is lively, inquisitive and amusing to observe. Its movements are often acrobatic.

Description:
Size: 10 cm (4 in)
COCK:
Body: dark olive brown. Nape of neck: yellow. Chest and belly: greyish-white. Crest: dark brown. Beak and legs: brown.
HEN:
Identical, so this bird cannot be sexed by appearance. Cock birds are aggressive in defence of their territory chasing off larger birds very actively, and their behaviour is the best way of determining sex.

Diet: (Softbill)
Ixulus often take a nectar mixture of honey and water to excess and ignore other essential nutrients, unless discouraged. Their diet must be carefully monitored. Soft fruit such as pears, grapes and berries should be provided together with fine grade insectile mix and small live insects. Sponge cake soaked in honey and water is enjoyed. Houseflies and blowflies are eagerly devoured, but maggots and mealworms often prove too tough skinned for this small species.

This bird must be carefully acclimatised and needs housing in a warm conservatory in cold weather, as it tends to be be rather delicate.

A pair of Yellow-Collared Ixulus

Breeding:
This is a difficult species to breed, and patience is required. Accommodation with plenty of cover is needed to encourage breeding. Preferred nesting sites are similar to those chosen by the Black-Chinned Yuhina. Shrubs and climbing plants with fine grasses and roots are used for nesting material.

A maximum clutch numbers three eggs and the incubation period is around 16 days. Plenty of small livefood is necessary for rearing the young.

JAVA SPARROW ◄◇
Padda oryzivora
Origin: Indonesia

A good choice for the novice bird keeper, this hardy species may live for many years with the minimum of care and attention. Once acclimatised, the Java Sparrow can be kept in an outside aviary all year round.

The smooth shiny plumage of the Java Sparrow rarely looks untidy or ruffled. Feather condition in this species indicates the state of health and ruffled feathers often suggest illness. If in doubt, consult your veterinary surgeon.

It is advisable to keep a Java Sparrow with birds of fairly average size such as weavers, whydahs and Cut-Throat Finches and not with small waxbills. In large aviaries however, many fanciers do keep this species mixed with Zebra Finches and other similar birds.

There are now several colour forms of the Java Sparrow, the original grey, and

A pair of Java Sparrows

white, fawn and pied. The description below applies to the grey bird.

Description:
Size: 13 cm (5½ in)
COCK:
Head and tail: black. Cheeks: white. Body: dove-grey. There is an eye ring of red, bare skin. Beak: pink. Legs: pinkish-beige.
HEN:
Alike. Sexing cannot be done by appearance, so watch for display behaviour.

Diet: (Seedeater)
Mixed millets and plain canary seed form the basic diet. Hemp is also appreciated, as is greenfood. Grit and cuttlefish bone must always be available.

Breeding:
These birds breed in a typical manner. Boxes or baskets are often used.

PILEATED JAY △
Cyanocorax affinis
Origin: South America

As with many of the jay family, the Pileated Jay is inquisitive, active and something of a clown, and can become very tame. It may be housed with other large softbills, doves and pheasants, but not when other birds are breeding as it often robs nests taking eggs or chicks.

Description:
Size: 36 cm (14 in)
COCK:
Head: black. Throat and chest: black. Nape of neck: blue-white. Upperparts: brownish-blue. Belly: white. Moustache streak: blue. Beak: black. Legs: grey.
HEN:
Alike. Hard to sex by appearance, so observe behaviour.

Diet: (Softbill)

Coarse grade insectile mix mixed with minced beef forms the basis of the diet. The remainder of the menu should comprise mixed fruits, mealworms, maggots and some soaked raisins, sultanas and perhaps a little sponge. Mealworms are a great aid in taming. An occasional frozen dead chick or mouse should be purchased for feeding to this Jay.

Breeding:

The Pileated Jay is a difficult bird to breed. Pairs are cautious about nesting and need plenty of seclusion and space. They may be provided with a well covered open fronted nest box, but occasionally they may be tempted to construct their own untidy nest in a bush. Three to five eggs form the normal clutch and the incubation period lasts three weeks. Sadly they frequently devour their own young after they hatch. A plentiful supply of livefood, particularly small mice, may help to discourage them from this practice.

WHITE-CRESTED LAUGHING THRUSH △
Garrulax leucolophus
Origin: India

A bold, amusing bird which is very entertaining in a large aviary. It may be mixed with other starlings and thrushes, but should not be housed with smaller types or very timid birds. It is also rather noisy.

Description:

Size: 30 cm (12 in)

COCK:

Back: chestnut-brown. Wings and tail: darker brown. Head, crest and chest: white. Face: sports a black mask. Beak: black. Legs: gun-metal grey.

HEN:

Similar, making it difficult to pick a true pair, although its crest is smaller than that of the cock.

Diet: (Softbill)

Coarse grade insectile mixture and raw minced beef should be fed two or three times a week. Livefood is also necessary. Mixed fruit of all kinds should form about 40% of the menu, and insectile mixture

A pair of Pileated Jays

A White-Crested Laughing Thrush

should be sprinkled over diced fruit.

This species becomes very hardy after acclimatisation and can be kept outside, needing only a dry, frost-proof shelter, free from damp and draughts. It often attempts to roost outside even in cold weather, but should be discouraged from doing so.

Breeding:
Few successful breeding results have been recorded, but this should not deter the keen fancier from trying. Try to provide a secluded aviary and plenty of livefood for rearing the young.

LAVENDER FINCH ●
Lagonosticta caerulescens
Origin: West Africa

This is a lively finch with quick movements, which makes a peaceful yet interesting addition to a mixed aviary. However, it also has a tendency to pluck its own feathers and also those of its companions. For this reason, it is recommended that only one pair of this species be kept. A lone pair do not pluck each other quite so readily as several kept together. This species becomes tame very quickly and has a quiet murmuring song, which is repeated quite frequently as it settles down to roost.

Description:
Size: 13 cm (5 in)
COCK:
Body: Grey. Rump: scarlet. Beak: dark grey. Legs: dark grey.
HEN:
Similar, but the grey plumage appears slightly muted and is often more smokey-brown in tone. The hen is slightly smaller.

Diet: (Seedeater)
Mixed millets form the basic diet. Greenfood, spray millet and some livefood such as fresh ants' eggs should be provided. Grit and cuttlefish bone must always be available.

This species needs protection from severe weather in an indoor flight but extra heat is not necessary.

Although it often looks very scruffy when offered for sale because of its habit of feather plucking, this should not deter a prospective buyer. It does not indicate poor health. Once installed in an aviary, the bird should soon improve.

Breeding:
A Lavender Finch pair nests happily in a nest box with a small round entrance hole or in a globular wicker basket, and sometimes the birds build their own nest in a bush. Plenty of nesting material should be provided including soft grasses, moss, wool and feathers. The hen lays four to five round white eggs and incubation usually lasts about 12 days. The young fledge in 14 days.

Soaked seed, egg rearing food and soaked bread should be provided for rearing the young. Extra supplies of fresh ants' eggs should be given.

Occasionally the Lavender Finch hybridises with the Fire Finch, if housed in the same aviary. This produces a hybrid which is very attractive in appearance.

The Lavender Finch can be allowed free flight outside the aviary during the breeding season, once a nest has been completed, as it returns to feed its young.

BLACK-HEADED ○ ■
MANNIKIN
Lonchura malacca atricapilla
Origin: India

The Black-Headed Mannikin is very easy to manage, but not a bird from which to expect spectacular breeding results. It is one of the most popular species with beginners, since it is so hardy. It is peaceful and it does not disturb others in a mixed collection of birds of similar size and habits. A glossy Black-Headed Mannikin often does well on the show bench.

Description:
Size: 10 cm (5 in)
COCK:
Head: black. Neck and throat: black. Body: chestnut. Wings and tail: chestnut. Belly: black. Beak: silver-grey. Legs: grey.
HEN:
Similar, but cannot be sexed by appearance so, observe behaviour.

Diet: (Seedeater)
Mixed millets and plain canary seed form the basic diet. Spray millet, seeding grasses and greenfood are enjoyed. Grit and cuttlefish bone must always be available.

Breeding:
Breeding this species is a challenge for the fancier, but is worth the extra effort. A pair must be provided with sprouted seed, seeding grasses, extra millet sprays and plenty of small livefood. Some

Opposite: a Lavender Finch

MAGPIE MANNIKIN ◀ ◇
Amauresthes fringilloides
Origin: South Africa and West Africa

This attractive large Mannikin is very hardy and can remain outside all year round. It should be housed with larger birds or those who are aggressive and able to defend themselves, since it can be quarrelsome and has a heavy beak which can inflict injuries. It thrives with Java Sparrows, weavers and whydahs. A well matched pair of Magpie Mannikins with similar markings often does well on the show bench.

Above: a Black-Headed Mannikin

Above right: a Magpie Mannikin

mashed hard boiled egg may be fed and fresh ants' eggs are eagerly taken.

Nest baskets should be placed in good, thick cover. Alternatively twigs and coarse grasses may be fixed up in thick bushes to tempt a pair to constuct their own bulky, dome-shaped nest. Three to four eggs form a normal clutch and the incubation period is around 13 days.

In the past, this species has always been readily available and inexpensive to purchase, so many fanciers have not tried to breed it. It is now less frequently available and should therefore be encouraged to breed. Hybrids have been recorded between this species and Bengalese, Spice Birds and White-Headed Mannikins.

It likes to perch and roost in high places in the aviary and shelter, and a group often sit together in a long line.

Description:
Size: 10 to 13 cm (4 to 5 in)
COCK:
Head: black. Back, wings and tail: brown. Underparts: white. Beak: top mandible: black; lower mandible, grey. Legs: black.
HEN:
Alike. May not be sexed by appearance, so it is best to purchase several birds and allow them to pair themselves.

Diet: (Seedeater)
Plain canary seed and mixed millets form the basic diet. Spray millet is enjoyed. Greenfood is appreciated by certain Magpie Mannikins, but ignored by others. Grit and cuttlefish bone are essential.

Breeding:
Several pairs may be housed together in a

large aviary for breeding purposes, since they are colony breeders in the wild state. Odd birds should be removed.

Pairs construct a nest in open-fronted nest boxes or globular wicker baskets. They use whatever materials are available, including grasses, leaves and twigs, forming an entrance passage into the nest.

Four to six eggs are laid and the birds take turns in sitting for the 12-day incubation period. Chicks may be reared on dry seed alone, but sprouted seed should be provided with extra millet sprays, chopped mealworms, ants' eggs and soaked stale bread for extra nourishment.

The young commence their juvenile moult at around 12 weeks of age, but often do not attain full adult plumage until they are one year of age. They are rather slow developers.

WHITE-HEADED MANNIKIN
Lonchura maja
Origin: Indonesia

○ ■

This bird is ideal for the novice fancier, as it has a particularly friendly disposition. It is hardy enough to be kept outside all year round and frequently lives for over ten years. Even when breeding, this species is tolerant and peaceful with other seedeaters of similar size and habits, and its ease of management makes it an excellent choice for the beginner.

Description:
Size: 13 cm (5 in)
COCK:
Body: chocolate brown. Head: white.

A pair of White-Headed Mannikins

Beak: greyish-blue. Legs: grey. Eyes: black.
HEN:
Similar, but the head and beak are smaller than those of the cock.

Diet: (Seedeater)
Mixed millets and greenfood form the basic diet. If available, an occasional mealworm is enjoyed. Grit and cuttlefish bone must always be available.

Breeding:
It is sometimes a little difficult to get pairs to start breeding, but once accomplished, this bird rears young very well. An average clutch is four eggs with an incubation period of 12 days.

Rearing food should be provided in the form of soaked bread and a few chopped mealworms, if available, together with the normal seed diet. The young fledge in 25 days and the parents continue to feed them for some time afterwards. This species is often cross-bred with Bengalese.

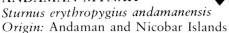

ANDAMAN MYNAH ◆ △
Sturnus erythropygius andamanensis
Origin: Andaman and Nicobar Islands

The Andaman Mynah is a lively, inquisitive bird which makes an interesting aviary species. A single bird or a pair can safely be kept in an aviary containing similar types, such as other mynahs, Cedar Waxwings, starlings, jays and Pekin Robins, without aggression. The Andaman Mynah is easy to tame and can be taught to take mealworms from the hand. Although not brightly coloured, it does show to advantage in an aviary, as it contrasts well with more gaudy birds. It is a good exhibition species.

Right: an Andaman Mynah

Opposite page: a Pagoda Mynah

Description:
Size: 20 cm (8 in)
COCK:
Head: white. Breast: white merging into light grey underneath. Back: light grey. Rump: white. Wings: black with a green sheen on outer flights. Tail: black tipped with white. Beak and legs: Yellow. Eyes: white.
HEN:
Identical. Difficult to sex by appearance, so observe behaviour.

Diet: (Softbill)
Insectile mix, fruit and fresh ants' eggs form the basic diet. Occasional mealworms should be provided, but too many make this bird grow fat. This species sometimes picks up and eats a little millet seed.

The Andaman Mynah likes to bathe, so a pool in the aviary is welcomed, and it chatters and calls excitedly as it splashes around.

It can stand extremes of heat and cold, but needs protection from frosty conditions so provide a shelter that is free from draughts.

Breeding:
Few captive breedings have been recorded for this bird. Plenty of livefood must be provided, if breeding is to be encouraged. Mealworms and fresh ants' eggs should be mixed with soil and sand in a bowl. A piece of freshly dug turf is much enjoyed, turned over so it may be picked at. Plenty of cover and a selection of nest sites are needed.

PAGODA MYNAH ◆ △
Sturnus pagodarum
Origin: India and Sri Lanka

This small mynah may be kept outside all year round after acclimatisation and does not require a great deal of space. It is confident and bold and can be a little aggressive when kept in pairs. A single bird mixes well with other similar sized softbills, but keep a close watch on pairs to see no fighting occurs with other aviary inhabitants. A single bird becomes very tame with its owner. This engaging bird often imitates the call sounds of other birds with great skill.

Description:

Size: 20 cm (8 in)

COCK:

Head and crest: black. Face, neck and stomach: buff. Shoulders and wings: grey-blue merging into dark grey. Tail: dark brown with a white tip. Beak: yellow with a blue base beneath the nostril area. Legs: greenish-yellow.

HEN:

Very similar to the cock, but sometimes a little smaller with a shorter crest.

Diet: (Softbill)

Its diet is similar to that of the Andaman Mynah. Coarse grade insectile mixture should be combined with a wide variety of diced fruit. Livefood is necessary and berries, soaked raisins and sultanas are enjoyed. Raw beef can provide variety.

Breeding:

A large box or log situated in a quiet corner encourages this species to construct a rather untidy, large nest. A shelf in the bird room or shelter is often selected. A tame bird is inclined to build a more visible nest. Try to provide a variety of nesting material such as long grasses, mosses and any feathers available from the aviary.

A clutch of three or four eggs is normal. Mealworms and ants' eggs help in chick rearing.

ROTHSCHILD'S MYNAH ◆ △
Leucopsar rothschildi
Origin: Bali

This truly beautiful softbill is sometimes called a mynah, a starling or a grackle, which can be rather confusing. It is very attractive, easily tamed and simple to feed. It may be housed with other similar sized softbills with safety.

Description:

Size: 25 cm (10 in)

COCK:

Head (including crest): white. Body: white. A wide area of blue-green bare skin surrounds eyes, covers lores and extends to sides of neck. Beak: creamy-grey. Legs: pale grey. Black tips on wings and tail.

HEN:

Similar, but smaller and slimmer.

Diet: (Softbill)

This species enjoys proprietary brand mynah pellets. Diced fruit of all kinds should be given and may be coated with coarse grade insectile mixture. Raw meat is also appreciated.

This hardy bird thrives in a large aviary with a shelter which does not have to be heated. It can withstand quite low temperatures. It loves to bathe and takes a great pride in its appearance, regularly grooming its white feathers.

Breeding:

Plenty of cover should be provided to encourage pairs to make an attempt at breeding. Although few captive breedings have been recorded, there is evidence that this species does go to nest if the conditions are suitable.

A selection of nest sites should be available including boxes, logs and large baskets filled with straw. Livefood is necessary if young are produced.

A Rothschild's Mynah

BOURKE'S PARRAKEET ☐

Neophema bourkii
Origin: Central Australia

This attractive parakeet is one of the few parrotlike birds that may be safely kept in a mixed collection with small seedeaters or softbills. Its colouring is attractive despite its subdued tones. It breeds quite happily in a mixed aviary, and does not display any aggression. It does not require a large aviary, is hardy and can winter outside without heat if provided with a dry, frost-proof shelter.

Description:
Size: 23 cm (9 in)
COCK:
Beak: black. Upperparts: greyish-brown. Forehead: pale blue. Breast and underside: pinkish-brown. Wings and tail: tinged with violet blue. Legs: greyish-brown.

HEN:
Very similar, but there is little or no blue on the forehead.

Diet: (Seedeater)
Plain canary seed, mixed millets, hulled oats and groats, a small amount of sunflower seed and occasional hemp form the basic diet. Spray millet and seeding grasses are both relished and greenfood, such as dandelion and chickweed, should be offered. Grit and cuttlefish bone must always be available.

Breeding:
This species makes use of boxes or hollow logs. Three to six eggs are laid and incubation lasts about 18 days. Wood shavings or turf should be placed in the base of the nest box or log. The young are fed on the normal seed diet, but seeding grasses are eagerly taken. Plenty of greenfood should be available.

Bourke's Parrakeets

ELEGANT GRASS PARRAKEET ☐

Neophema elegans
Origin: South and West Australia

The Elegant Grass Parrakeet may be kept safely with other birds, except during the breeding season when it is wiser to house it alone, unless in a large aviary.

Description:
Size: 23 cm (9 in)
COCK:
Body: olive green. Forehead: bears a deep cobalt-blue band, edged with light blue. Wings: exhibit these same two shades on their edges. Throat and chest: greenish-yellow. Belly: yellow. Beak: charcoal grey. Legs: greyish-brown.
HEN:
Similar, but all the colour tones are much paler so they can be sexed easily.

Diet: (Seedeater)
Mixed millets and plain canary seed with a small amount of sunflower and hemp seed form the basic diet. Seeding grasses, regular supplies of greenfood, grit and cuttlefish bone should be provided.

This bird is easily managed and does not require a large flight unless kept with others for breeding. A sunny, warm aviary suits it well but some shade is necessary to prevent sun stroke. A dry, frost-proof shelter should be provided for cold weather. It is not quite as hardy as some parrotlike species.

Breeding:
Place nest boxes and hollow logs in the accommodation. The Elegant Grass Parrakeet requires a slightly larger nest box than a budgerigar. The cock bird's courtship display is amusing to watch as he performs a head bobbing dance accompanied by a twittering song.

The hen lays four to five eggs which she incubates for 18 to 21 days. Sprouted seed should be provided for the parents to rear the brood. This is the only necessary addition to the normal seed diet. Parents even rear their young on hard seed.

Chicks are ready to leave the nest in approximately 28 to 34 days. Young Elegant Grass Parrakeets are very shy when they first leave the nest, so make sure there are plenty of bushes in the aviary to provide cover for the timid youngsters and they soon gain confidence.

An Elegant Grass Parrakeet hen in poor feather condition

PLUM-HEADED PARRAKEET ☐
Psittacula cyanocephala
Origin: India and Sri Lanka

Tolerant of other birds, this species may be housed with some of the larger seedeaters, such as cardinals and other gentle natured parrotlike types, such as the cockatiel. This species is hardy and remains outside all year round, if a frost-proof shelter is provided.

Description:
Size: 36 cm (14 in)
COCK:
Head: rose pink. Throat and neck ring: black. Upper parts: green. Breast: yellowish-green. Shoulder patch: dark red. Wings and tail show some blue and yellow feathers. Beak: orange-red. Legs: grey.
HEN:
Similar, but her head is blue-grey, her beak yellow and her body does not have the red shoulder patches.

Diet: (Seedeater)
Plain canary seed, mixed millets, sunflower seed, peanuts and a little hemp form the basic diet. This bird enjoys apple and plenty of greenfood. Grit and cuttlefish bone must always be provided.

Breeding:
Since young cock birds resemble adult hens, it is best to purchase a fully mature pair if possible when hoping to breed. Single hens are sometimes rather difficult to obtain.

Pairs usually breed best in separate accommodation but can be bred in a mixed aviary, if it is fairly large.

Nest boxes should be slightly larger in size than the normal budgerigar box, although some Plum-Head pairs use this size. Boxes should be hung fairly high with space left on top to allow the bird to sit and guard the nest. Nesting material should consist of sawdust and wood shavings. This should be provided in the base of the boxes.

Four to six eggs are laid which the hen incubates alone. She does not leave the nest until the eggs have hatched and the chicks are ten days old. The cock bird feeds the hen and chicks from the time the eggs are

A Plum-Headed Parrakeet

laid. Hard boiled egg, soaked bread, ants' eggs, mealworms and soaked and sprouted seeds should be supplied.

Plum-Heads are shy breeders and abandon their nests if disturbed, so nests should not be inspected.

RED-RUMPED PARRAKEET ☐
Psephotus haematonotus
Origin: Australia

This is one of the most popular species of Australian parrakeets, because it is hardy and simple to feed, and therefore easy to keep. Breeding results are normally good. However, take great care when attempting to keep this species with other birds, as it can be very spiteful. If in doubt, keep a pair alone. In any case, it is best to have only one pair in a mixed collection.

Description:
Size: 28 cm (11 in)
COCK:
Body: varying shades of green. Stomach:

yellow. Wings: edged with dark blue. Rump: red. Beak: black. Legs: grey.

HEN:

Does not have the red rump and is generally less distinctive in colour. Beak: grey.

Diet: (Seedeater)

Plain canary seed, mixed millets, sunflower, hemp (if available), groats and oats form the basic diet. This species enjoys greenfood and loves apple. Grit and cuttlefish bone must always be available.

A spacious aviary is required with a dry, frost- and damp-proof shelter for bad weather. Plenty of wing exercise is important.

Breeding:

For those fanciers inexperienced in breeding birds, the Red-Rumped Parrakeet is a good choice, as pairs require the minimum of supervision. A pair nests very readily if a large nest box is provided. Rotting wood should be placed in the base to a depth of 10 cm (4 in).

A normal clutch of eggs numbers between four and seven. The incubation period is 21 days with the hen sitting alone. The parents rear their young with very few additions to the normal diet, but try to provide soaked and sprouted seeds.

The young fledge in one month and may be left with the parents for a further two or three weeks until the hen begins another round. They should be removed at the first sign of this, or the cock may attack the fledglings.

SPLENDID GRASS PARRAKEET ☐

Noephema splendida
Origin: Australia

This parrakeet is peaceful and tolerant even during the breeding season and may safely be housed with Bourke's Parrakeet and/or the cockatiel, although it is keener to breed, if kept on its own. It is much sought for its beautiful colours.

Description:

Size: 23 cm (9 in)

COCK:

Head: Deep blue. Upperparts: green. Stomach: yellow. Chest: red. Wings: green

with blue and black feathers. Tail: green with black and yellow feathers. Eyes: brown. Legs: blackish-brown. Beak: black.

HEN:

No blue on head or red on chest. Underside: olive green, and brown above.

Diet: (Seedeater)

Plain canary seed, mixed millets, sunflower seed and oats form the basic diet. Greenfood and apple are appreciated. Grit and cuttlefish bone must always be available.

A spacious aviary with a dry, frost-proof shelter should be provided, with protection from harsh winds.

Left: a pair of Red-Rumped Parrakeets

Opposite page: a Splendid Grass Parrakeet cock

Breeding:

Large next boxes, slightly deeper than those liked by buderigars, should be placed in the quarters. Pairs are usually quite eager to go to nest.

A clutch of eggs may number up to seven. The incubation period is 19 days and both parents share in sitting and rearing. When the young fledge they resemble the hen. Young cock birds soon sprout a few red feathers around the base of the neck and some blue on the head. Two rounds of eggs per breeding season are acceptable.

TURQUOISINE GRASS PARRAKEET ☐

Neophema pulchella
Origin: New South Wales, Victoria and South Australia

This brightly coloured parrakeet is easy to manage, feed and breed. It may be kept with other parrotlike species, such as Bourke's Parrakeet or the Elegant Grass

Above: a Turquoisine Grass Parrakeet

Opposite page: a Pin-Tailed Parrot Finch

Diet: (Seedeater)

Mixed millets, plain canary seed and sunflower seed form the basic diet. Greenfood and a liberal quantity of maw seed are appreciated. Soaked and sprouted seeds should be fed at all times. Grit and cuttlefish bone must always be provided.

Breeding:

The courtship display of the cock includes a soft whistling song. Nest boxes should be provided for breeding pairs and they often use a budgerigar nesting box. The base should be filled with damp moss or wood pulp.

Four to five eggs are laid and the hen incubates alone. The incubation period is 17 to 19 days. The cock bird feeds her while she is sitting and for a further few days after the chicks have hatched. Both parents then feed the young. Rearing food should include soaked and sprouted seeds, soaked bread, greenfood and maw seed. Young birds should not be allowed to breed until they attain two years of age. This species has cross-bred with the Elegant Grass Parrakeet.

PIN-TAILED PARROT FINCH ○ ■

Erythrura prasina
Origin: India and Indonesia

A rather timid and nervous bird that requires careful acclimatisation, but thrives well if given a little extra attention. Once established in a well planted aviary, it lives outside without any difficulty. It mixes well with other seedeaters of similar size and is not aggressive, but needs plenty of space in which to exercise, as it has a tendency to gain too much weight.

Description:

Size: 13 cm (5 in)

COCK:

Body: green. Face and throat: blue. Lower breast, tail and rump: bright red. Long pointed central tail feathers. Beak: black. Legs: cream.

HEN:

Similar, but no blue on face or red on lower parts. The hen also has a much shorter tail. The immature cock bird resembles a hen so care is needed when purchasing a pair.

Parrakeet, if the aviary is fairly large. It becomes active in the evening, but is quiet and lethergic during the day. It needs plenty of flying space despite its tendency to inactivity during the day. A frost-proof shelter is required for bad weather.

Description:

Size: 20 cm (8 in)

COCK:

Body: green. Lores and cheeks: turquoise-blue. Throat and chest: yellow. Wings: blue and chestnut red. Beak: horn colour. Legs: yellowish-grey.

HEN:

Similar, but duller colours. No chestnut red on wings. Less blue on face.

Diet: (Seedeater)

Plain canary seed and mixed millets form the basic diet. Greenfood and sprouted seed are enjoyed. Grit and cuttlefish bone are essential. This species often needs unpolished rice during the acclimatisation period as it sometimes refuses other food, but later canary seed often proves the favourite seed.

Breeding:

The cock bird performs a very interesting courting dance, circling the hen and jerking his tail up and down while uttering a few strange noises.

The nest may be built in a box, in a bush or under some form of cover. More than one pair of this species can be kept in a mixed collection, as fighting is unlikely.

Four to five eggs form an average clutch. The incubation period is 13 days and both parents take turns in sitting on the eggs. Try to provide plentiful supplies of soaked seed and a few mealworms and ants' eggs, which are needed for rearing healthy chicks.

PARSON FINCH ○ ■

Poephila cincta
Origin: Australia

This beautifully marked finch resembles the Long-Tailed/Heck's Grassfinch, but has a short tail with a black beak and red legs. It has a similar disposition although, in general, it is more docile. This species may be kept with the Long-Tailed/Heck's in pairs, if the aviary is fairly large. It is hardy, but as with all Australian finches needs a little more warmth in cold weather. A dry, damp- and draught-proof shelter is required with a heater if the temperature is below 14°C (57°F).

Description:

Size: 10 to 13 cm (4 to 5 in)

COCK:

Head: dove-grey. Stomach: buff. Bib: black. Black mask across eyes. Wings: light brown. Legs: red. Beak: black.

HEN:

Identical, but sometimes the black bib is a little smaller, but this is not always a reliable indication of sex.

Diet: (Seedeater)

Plain canary seed, mixed millets, spray millet and some greenfood form the basic diet. Soaked and sprouted seed should be fed fairly regularly to keep this species in first class condition. Grit and cuttlefish bone must always be available.

Breeding:

This bird likes to choose its own partner and pair bonding is very srong. Try to purchase several birds and once partners are selected use plastic split rings to identify each pair.

Several nest boxes should be provided for each pair so that there is a wide selection for them to inspect. The cock Parson Finch constructs a nest skilfully, but often tears it apart once completed and rebuilds in a different spot in the aviary with the same material. This habit may be due to a feeling of insecurity. The hen selects grass as the chosen nesting material and searches for it herself. Pairs also like to use white material, such as feathers or wool, dragging it into the nest to make a lining.

Little addition to the normal diet is required and livefood is not necessary. Four to five white eggs are laid and both parents share in the incubation, which commences after the third egg has been laid. The chicks hatch in around 12 days. The young birds fledge in 22 to 24 days but return to the nest to roost each evening. At six weeks of age they should be fully independent and must be removed from their parents to make way for the next clutch of eggs.

A pair of Parson Finches in an aviary

A Pekin Robin

PEKIN ROBIN   ◇◆
Leiothrix lutea
Origin: China

The colourful, smoothly plumaged and lively Pekin Robin fits into a mixed collection of birds including even small finches, but is sometimes intolerant of its own kind. Therefore, only a single pair or a cock bird should be kept in an aviary. Avoid keeping this bird in a collection where smaller birds are breeding, however, as the Pekin Robin has a nasty tendency to rob the nests and eat the eggs. If breeding only birds of a larger size than the Pekin Robin then the problem does not arise, since it is reticent about attempting such interference.

Since this bird loves to bathe, try to include a small pool in the aviary.

The Pekin is a hardy type and winters well, taking moults in its stride. It may be left outside provided there is a dry, frost-proof shelter available.

This bird is easily tamed.

Description:
Size: 15 cm (6 in)

COCK:
Body: brownish-green. Wings: brown with red. Eye: black. Eye ring: cream. Beak: orange. Breast: yellowish-orange. Legs: cream.

HEN:
Similar, but much duller. Try to listen for the melodious song of the cock as this is the best method of sexing this bird.

Diet: (Softbill)
Fine grade insectile mix, fruit, greenfood and about six mealworms per day form the basic diet. It also takes a little seed on occasions, if housed with seedeaters. This bird should be given a variety of insects as available. It has quite a small appetite.

Breeding:
Pairs construct a deep cup-shaped nest of reeds, bark, moss and fine small twigs. Linings of moss should be placed in the base of nest boxes for them. The boxes should be provided in a secluded position high up in dense vegetation. Between three to five eggs are laid and incubation lasts 13 days. The young fledge some 12 days after hatching. They are dependent on their parents for several further weeks.

CALIFORNIA QUAIL □◀
Lophortyx californicus
Origin: California, U.S.A.

A very hardy and easily managed ground bird, which adds interest to the aviary at ground level and lives happily with such types as cockatiels and budgerigars or weavers, whydahs and Java Sparrows. The California Quail can be aggressive, so no more than one pair should be kept in an aviary. It must not be kept with smaller birds.

Description:
Size: 25 cm (10 in)
COCK:
Head: black and white patterned. Breast: grey. Underparts: buff with black pattern. Crest: black, angled forward. Beak: black. Legs: black.
HEN:
Lacks black and white pattern on head and has a shorter crest of brown feathers. Body as cock.

Diet: (Seedeater)
Mixed millets, crushed maize and oats, a little insectile mix, mealworms and ants' eggs form the basic diet. Other available insects should be fed and a little soaked bread is also enjoyed. Thick vegetation in the aviary encourages this bird to eat insects.

Plenty of ground cover and a dry shelter are necessary for this species. This bird is very susceptible to damp and should be enclosed in very wet weather. It likes to perch high off the ground on occasion and suitable branches should be provided in a quiet spot. California Quail, in common with other quail species, may take fright easily, particularly at night. Roosting spots should be screened with thick bushes or conifers to prevent sudden alarms.

Breeding:
In order to nest, California Quail need clumps of heather or low growing shrubs and long grass. A hen is capable of laying up to 20 eggs, which she incubates alone. This hen does not always incubate her eggs properly and sometimes it may be necessary to use a domestic Bantam hen as a foster mother.

A good rearing mixture for chicks is hard boiled egg mixed with crumbled

A California Quail

A beautiful silver mutation of the Chinese Painted Quail

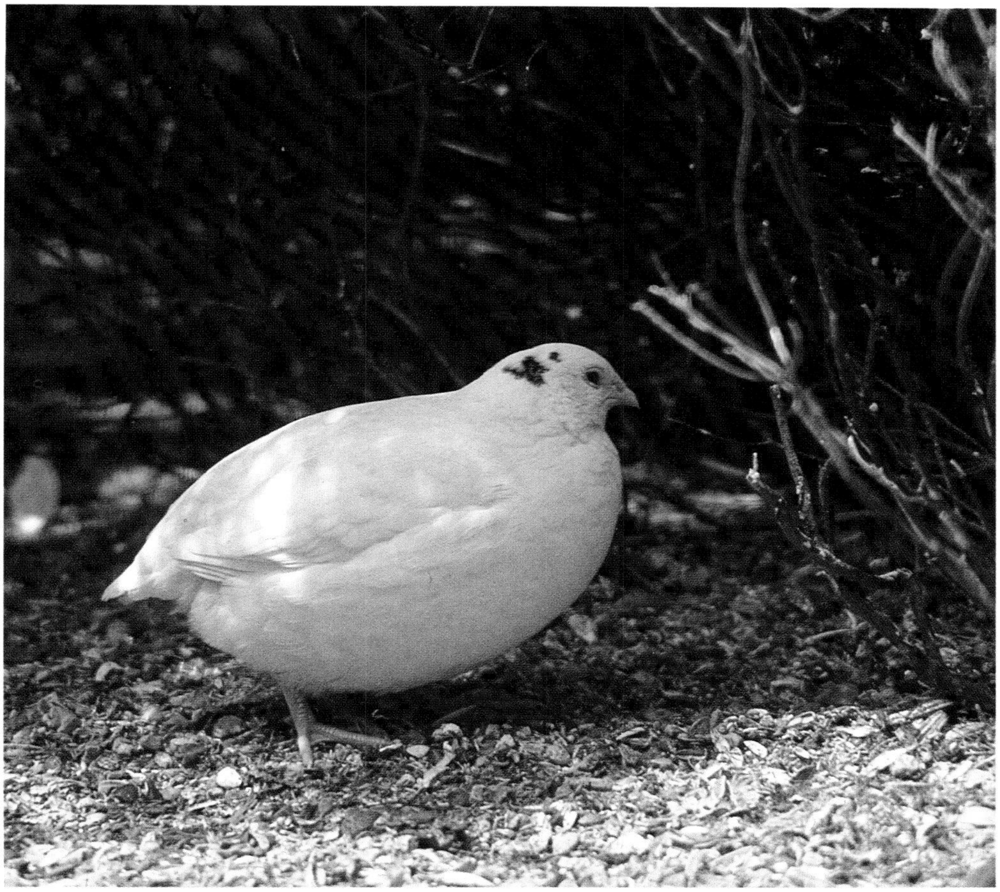

rusks. Minced raw meat, chopped greenfood, ants' eggs and a variety of insects should be provided. Breadcrumbs may be added to minced meat and placed in a separate dish. Sand, grit and cuttlefish bone should be available at all times.

California Quail chicks grow rapidly and are independent in a few weeks. They may be left with their parents until the cocks attain the adult plumage of patterned colouring, when they should be removed as the cock bird may then show aggression to the other males.

CHINESE PAINTED QUAIL ●○■

Excalfactoria chinensis
Origin: Southern Asia

This is a beautiful miniature quail which prospers well in a mixed aviary in company with other small birds. It performs a useful service by eating waste seed from the ground. Only one pair of Chinese Painted Quail should be kept per aviary, as they are intolerant of their own kind and fighting may occur.

Description:
Size: 13 cm (5 in)
COCK:
Head: mottled with a black and white pattern. Body: brown mottled with black and beige. Breast: blue-grey. Beak: black. Legs: yellow.
HEN:
Body: dull brown, mottled with black. Breast: pale brown. Lacks patterned head of the cock.

Diet: (Seedeater)
Mixed millets and plain canary seed form the basic diet. Maw seed is also enjoyed. Greenfood should be given and some livefood, preferably small insects. The Chinese Painted Quail forages actively in the aviary for insects and usually manages to find plenty on its own. An area of thick grass should be provided; this will give the bird a supply of insects and also a source of cover.

During cold weather this species should be placed in an indoor enclosure, but does not require heat.

Breeding:

A shallow hollow in the ground, concealed in thick vegetation, forms the nest site. Moss and leaves and blades of grass are placed in the depression to line the nest. Take care not to trample on the nest when entering the aviary.

The hen lays between six and eight eggs and incubates them alone, while the cock guards the nest against any interference, ferociously if needs be. The incubation period is 16 days. Upon hatching the chicks are immediately able to run about and do so during the first day. Again, care must be taken not to trample on them. At this age they can slip through even very small mesh. Place a board about 10 cm (4 in) around the bottom sides of their aviary to prevent this.

The chicks eat ants' eggs, finely chopped mealworms and lettuce. Insectile mix should be provided and sometimes a little raw minced meat. Chopped hard boiled egg is also useful, but remains must be cleared away before they spoil. The young also need plenty of ground egg shell, lime and grit.

The cock may not adapt well to fatherhood and may worry the hen while she is sitting on the eggs, or peck at the young chicks when they first appear. This sometimes happens with the first brood and can be attributed to inexperience. Should this happen, it is wise to remove the cock from the aviary. At four weeks the chicks are independent and should be taken away and the cock returned. The pair nest again for a second round. Somewhat shy birds, pairs do not always nest and rear well in their first season.

No more than three broods of chicks per year should be allowed, otherwise the hen is exhausted and inferior quality chicks are produced. Segregate the cock if he attempts persistent breeding.

RED-BILLED QUELEA ○ ◀ ◇

Quelea quelea
Origin: Africa

This species is a very suitable weaver for novice fanciers. If several pairs are kept, budgerigars, Cut-Throat Finches or Zebra Finches make suitable companions. One single pair is safe with smaller finches, if the accommodation is fairly large.

Description:

Size: 10 to 13 cm (4 to 5 in)
COCK:
Body: golden-brown with dark brown markings. Face: chocolate brown. Beak: red. There is a red rim around the eye. Legs: pinky-brown. The plumage of the cock bird turns dull after the breeding season.
HEN:
Has a pale yellow beak.

Diet: (Seedeater)

Mixed millets, spray millet and plenty of insect food and half-ripened grain, such as grass seed form the basic diet. Grit and cuttlefish bone must always be available.

This hardy bird can be kept in an outside flight all year round. However, ensure that the bird roosts in a shelter when moulting from nuptial plumage.

Breeding:

This bird is particularly difficult to breed. However, the cock is a very keen nest builder and is normally assisted by his mate. A ball-shape nest is constructed with an entrance at one side. Fresh grass is the preferred nest material, so new grass clippings should be provided. Pairs often build one nest, destroy it and then rebuild a new one right next to the first.

This weaver is a colony nester, so several pairs of birds may be kept to encourage breeding attempts. Despite the fact that pairs build plenty of nests, very few reports exist of successful captive breeding, so this bird presents a challenge to the keen fancier. Fighting it not likely unless the aviary is very small.

INDIAN BLUE ROLLER ◆ △
Coracias benghalensis
Origin: Asia

This medium sized softbill may be kept in harmony in a large aviary with other species, particularly jays, and several members of its own kind, providing that all rollers in a collection are introduced to their accommodation together. This bird is not aggressive with smaller species, despite its heavy build. However, it does sometimes emit rather harsh grating sounds which may not endear one to the neighbours! Fortunately, it usually only makes a noise at the beginning of the breeding season.

Description:
Size: 46 cm (13 in)

COCK:

Body: Greyish-blue and lilac. Head: turquoise-grey. Wings: turquoise and royal blue. Chest and cheeks: lavender. Throat: buff. Underparts: lavender fading to pale brown. The head appears very large.

HEN:

Very similar so cannot be sexed by appearance. Observe behaviour to distinguish between sexes.

Diet: (Softbill)
Coarse grade insectile mix, minced meat and mealworms form the basic diet. Locusts and crickets are relished. As much insect food as possible must be provided.

The name "roller" comes from the bird's habit of flying up high and swooping downwards with fast beating wings in a rolling type motion. This is normally observed only at the start of the breeding season. At other times this species appears quite lethargic, although this is deceptive since it can spot an insect and catch it with great speed. This bird particularly enjoys basking in sunshine on a high thin branch.

Breeding:
Few breeding results have been recorded in captivity, as it is often difficult to obtain a true pair. Try to purchase several birds as they may then pair themselves.

Nesting takes place high up in trees so it is difficult to provide the correct conditions in an aviary. Plenty of cover is required.

An Indian Blue Roller: despite its heavy build, it is not aggressive

AFRICAN SILVERBILL
Lonchura malabarica cantans
Origin: West and Central Africa

An adaptable, easy-to-breed species which also incubates the eggs of other birds and rears their young. Easily managed by the most inexperienced aviculturist, the African Silverbill has many other advantages. It is hardy and can withstand extremes of temperature. It lives happily with other small seedeaters.

There is also an Indian Silverbill (*Lonchura malabarica*) but this is not such a hardy bird as the African variety.

Description:
Size: 10 to 12 cm (4 to 4½ in)
COCK:
Head: creamy-brown. Body: creamy-brown. Wings: dark brown. Underparts: pale buff. Rump: black. Tail: black. Beak: silver. Legs: dull pink.
HEN:
Alike, so it is impossible to sex these birds by appearance. It is best to purchase several birds and allow them to choose their own mate. The cock has a pleasant song.

Diet: (Seedeater)
Plain basic canary seed and mixed millets form the basic diet. Millet sprays are also relished and occasional greenfood, grit and cuttlefish bone should be provided.

Breeding:
The African Silverbill has a very peaceful nature and happily breeds among other species of small bird, such as waxbills, in a mixed collection. Several pairs often nest at the same time and may help each other in the feeding of their chicks, once they are all out on the perches.

This bird may sometimes develop the unfortunate habit, shared with Zebra Finches, of making "sandwich nests". The bird constructs a nest, lays eggs and then immediately makes another nest on top. To prevent this, nest boxes or baskets should be filled with nesting material, tightly packed with a small amount of space left for the birds to complete their preparations. A quiet place must be selected for the nest boxes and baskets. The birds use soft materials such as mosses, soft grasses and feathers, constructing a narrow slip-in entrance to the nest.

Four eggs form the normal clutch and the incubation period is 12 days. While feeding the young, the parents should be given some extras such as soaked bread and hard boiled egg, some chopped mealworms and fresh ants' eggs. Soaked and sprouted seed is better than dry seed during the breeding season.

This bird hybridises with the Spice Bird quite frequently and is prepared to hatch and rear the young of restless sitters, such as the Cordon Bleu and the Red-Eared Waxbill.

This species also interbreed with Bengalese, so these can be used as foster parents in emergencies.

It is quite possible for one pair of African Silverbills to rear 20 young in one season. The group may all be left together to form a colony and true pairs may be identified with split plastic rings.

SPICE BIRD
Lonchura punctulata
Origin: India and Sri Lanka

The Spice Bird is one of the most popular of the mannikin family. Hardy and easy to manage, it is an ideal species for the novice fancier. It lives contentedly with other birds of a similar size in a mixed collection and can be safely housed with all the small waxbills.

Description:
Size: 13 cm (4½ in)
COCK:
Head: chocolate brown. Upperparts: brown. Underparts: white and each feather is edged with dark brown. Beak: grey. Legs: brownish-grey. Eyes: black. Tail: dark brown.
HEN:
Alike, so sexing can not be done by appearance. Listen for the unusual buzzing, humming song of the cock bird. If possible, purchase several birds to encourage them to select their own mates.

Diet: (Seedeater)
Plain canary seed and mixed millets form the basic diet. Millet sprays and greenfood are also enjoyed. Grit and cuttlefish bone must always be provided.

It can be housed outside throughout the

| Opposite: an African Silverbill

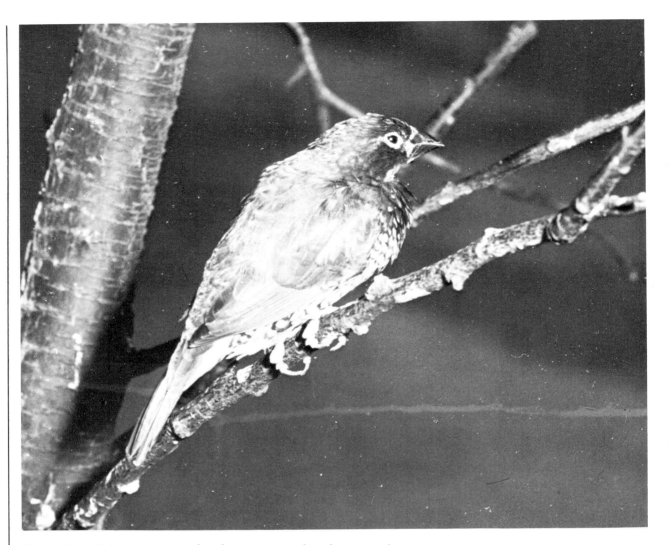

Above: a Spice Bird

Opposite: a Star Finch

year and only requires a dry, frost-proof shelter for roosting during winter months.

Breeding:
Spice Birds are not particularly keen breeders, but do go to nest under the right conditions. Nest boxes and wicker baskets should be provided in secluded places, such as shrubberies. Pairs make their own nests inside boxes or baskets with soft grasses, mosses and feathers. They desert their nests at the slightest noise or disturbance.

Four to eight eggs are laid and the incubation period is 13 days. The parents should be kept well supplied with sprouted seeds, millet sprays, greenfood and insects.

Should a pair fail to try and rear their young, Bengalese may be used as foster parents. Bengalese often interbreed with this species. They come from the same family (*Lonchura*). Parent-reared Spice Birds may be kept with their family to form a small colony.

STAR FINCH ● ○ ■
Bathilda ruficauda
Origin: Northern Australia

This is a popular Australian finch which is quite easy to breed. It is a peaceful natured species and mixes well with other birds in an aviary. During the breeding season, a pair may be transferred to separate accommodation where they are less likely to be disturbed.

Description:
Size: 13 cm (4½ in)

COCK:

Body: olive green. Breast: olive. Underparts: pale yellowish-green. Forehead: red. Cheeks and throat: red. Tail: brick red. Face and breast spotted with white dots. Beak: red. Legs: flesh.

HEN:

Similar, but less red on the face. It is

sometimes easy to mistake a young cock bird for a hen, if it has not attained full colour, so it is wise to try and obtain a mature, known pair for breeding.

Diet: (Seedeater)

Small plain canary seed and mixed millet form the basic diet. Greenfood and seeding grasses are enjoyed. Grit and cuttlefish bone must always be available.

As the Star Finch does not roost overnight in a nest box, it should be protected from cold and damp weather conditions. Bathing is enjoyed, so a pool should be provided, if possible.

Breeding:

A young hen often flies over her intended mate with a piece of grass in her beak, sometimes dragging it over his back. This is considered to be a preliminary ritual to "pair bonding".

Star Finches like to build their own nests in broom bushes interwoven with hay, but they do accept a nest box or a wicker basket, in which they will construct a dome-shaped nest of grass with a narrow entrance hole.

Pairs should not be allowed to breed until they are fully mature at two years of age. If a hen lays fertile eggs prior to this age, they may be removed and placed under Bengalese.

Egg binding is sometimes a problem with Star Finches, particularly if the weather is cold. They are also inclined to

leave the nest frequently instead of sitting on the eggs full time, so it is often better to place the pair in a flight by themselves to minimise disturbance.

Three to four round white eggs form the normal clutch and both parents incubate them during the day, although the hen usually sits for longer periods than the cock. Both birds occupy the nest at night. The eggs hatch in 12 to 14 days and the young are covered in fine white down. Star Finches are very attentive parents and do not seem to resent nest inspection, although this should always be kept to a minimum. The chicks leave the nest at 18 to 23 days and appear to be very shy at this stage. Three or four weeks later they should be independent and removed from their parents to allow for a further round. Immature birds are pale olive brown with a little red in the tail.

The juvenile moult occurs at between six weeks and eight months of age depending on how quickly the young mature, weather conditions and diet.

Although chick rearing pairs can be fed on hard seed alone, they benefit from sprouted seed, egg rearing food and insects.

A very strong pair bond is formed by Star Finch couples, so they should be rung with split plastic rings to make sure they are always kept together.

SUPERB SPREO STARLING △
Spreo superbus
Origin: East Africa

This is one of the most popular and beautiful of the glossy starling species. It has a very discordant cry, so is most often kept for its fabulous colour and ease of taming. It is a good exhibition species. Whilst a single bird does not harm those of other species, a pair can be spiteful and murderous. A pair kept for breeding needs to be kept in a separate flight. This species likes to bathe, so provide a pool in the aviary, if possible.

Description:

Size: 20 cm (8 in)
COCK:
Head: blue. Back: green. Chest and stomach: chestnut. Upper breast: blue. A white band separates these two colours. Beak: black. Legs: black.

A Superb Spreo Starling

HEN:

Alike. This species cannot be sexed by appearance, so observe behaviour.

Diet: (Softbill)

Coarse grade insectile mix, fruit and live-food fed every day form the basic diet. All fruit should be chopped up into cubes. Raisins, sultanas and currants are also enjoyed. Minced raw beef should be blended with the insectile mix, and all ingredients can be mixed together in one dish.

Breeding:

Supply a pair with a large nest box with an entrance hole near the top. Try to give plenty of nesting material including hay, dried grasses and roots. A large untidy nest is built completely filling the nest box.

Three to four eggs are laid and the incubation period lasts for 13 days. Plenty of livefood is required, including mealworms, maggots, smooth backed caterpillars and woodlice.

Chicks should be segregated from their parents as soon as they are able to feed themselves, or they may be attacked when a second round of eggs is laid.

PURPLE SUGARBIRD ◆
Cyanerpes caeruleus
Origin: Guyana

The Purple Sugarbird is one of the most attractive and brightly coloured of the sugarbird species. It is a delicate bird and must be carefully acclimatised. The Purple Sugarbird may be kept as a single pair with other small softbill or seedeating species. Several cock birds may be kept together with other birds. Do not keep more than one pair of sugarbirds with their own kind or other species, because fights may occur.

An indoor aviary in winter is a must and heat is required. In warm summer months, this sugarbird lives happily outside in a planted flight. It can live in captivity for 10 to 12 years under the right conditions.

Description:
Size: 13 cm (5 in)
COCK:

Body: purple-blue. Ear coverts: black. Wings, throat and tail: black. Beak: black. Legs and feet: yellow with black claws.

HEN:

Body: green. Throat: chestnut. Underparts: pale yellow with green markings. Throat has pale violet blue moustache markings at sides. Lores: chestnut. Beak: dark brown. Legs and feet: greenish-brown.

Diet: (Softbill)

Diet should be as varied as possible. Fine grade insectile mix should be fed together with a wide selection of fruit, including oranges, bananas and pears. It likes to feed on fruit suspended by stout thread near perching spots, which keeps the food clean and minimises fouling by droppings. Water mixed with just enough honey to colour it should be supplied in drinkers positioned well above ground level. Mealworms, fresh ants' eggs, hard boiled egg mash, cooked mashed potato and boiled rice mixed with honey are all enjoyed. Stale, soaked bread, sponge cake or rusks may be crumbled into a honey and water mix.

Breeding:

This species is not easy to breed. Nests are made of plant fibres suspended in tall bushes and a well planted conservatory may encourage a pair to go to nest.

Two or three small, white eggs are laid. The incubation period may vary between 14 and 21 days.

Moulting normally occurs twice a year, although cocks have been known to go an entire season without moulting at all.

A Purple Sugarbird hen

YELLOW-WINGED SUGARBIRD

Cyanerpes cyaneus
Origin: South America

This beautiful softbill is quite hardy once established and, like the Purple Sugarbird, it is sometimes called a honeycreeper. It can live for many years if given the correct type of care. A single pair agrees well with other small birds, but if several sugarbirds are kept, they should all be cock birds. If a hen is introduced, fights occur.

Description:
Size: 10 to 13 cm (4 to 5 in)
COCK (in nuptial plumage):
Body: bright cobalt-blue. Shoulders, wings, tail: black. Head: turquoise blue on crown. Beneath the wings is an area of yellow. Legs: red. The cock bird moults twice a year.
HEN:
Varying shades of olive green. Legs: creamy-brown. When not in nuptial plumage, the cock resembles the hen, but can always be distinguished by his red legs.

Diet: (Softbill)
As with the Purple Sugarbird, fine grade insectile mixture forms the basic diet. Fruit, such as pears, bananas and oranges, should be provided. Grapes, sultanas and raisins are relished. Large fruit should be suspended on a thread near a perch. Honey and water must be provided in a drinking tube.

This bird may be kept in an outdoor aviary when properly acclimatised, but is seen to best advantage in an indoor room setting (examples of which are shown in Chapter 1). It needs extra warmth in cold weather, and should not be submitted to extremes of temperature at any time. It loves to bathe and shows off to great advantage.

Breeding:
To encourage breeding, a pair must be provided with suitable nesting material in the form of soft grasses and mosses. The nest is most often constructed in a dense bush fairly high off the ground.

Two to three eggs are laid and the incubation period is 13 to 14 days. Plenty of small livefood is necessary for rearing.

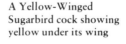

A Yellow-Winged Sugarbird cock showing yellow under its wing

BLUE-CAPPED TANAGER ◆
Thraupis cyanocephala
Origin: North western areas of South America

The Blue-Capped Tanager is one of the larger members of the many species in this family. Following proper acclimatisation, this colourful bird will live healthily in outdoor accommodation, becoming very hardy.

If a frost-proof shelter is provided, the Blue-Capped Tanager may winter outside or may be locked away at night depending on the weather.

Most tanagers become quite tame with their owners and take mealworms from the hand. They are very fond of bathing and a small pool affords endless pleasure and cleans the plumage of food and droppings.

This species is suitable for inclusion in a mixed collection with Pekin Robins, whydahs, bulbuls, fruitsuckers, and other birds of similar size and temperament.

Description:
Size: 20 cm (7½ in)
COCK:
Head: cobalt-blue. Back, wings and tail: black. Underparts: dark blue. Shoulders: golden-green. Forehead and eyes: black. Rump: yellow. Beak: black. Legs: dark horn.
HEN:
Alike. Behaviour gives the best indication of sex.

Diet: (Softbill)
Soft fruits, apples, grapes, oranges, pears and bananas form a large part of the basic diet. Fine grade insectile mix should be sprinkled on the fruit. Sponge cake soaked in nectar mixture is much enjoyed. Mealworms, well cleaned maggots, smooth, green caterpillars, grasshoppers and spiders all provide ideal livefood for this bird.

Breeding:
If breeding, remove this bird to a secluded, well planted aviary of its own. Wicker nest baskets should be hung in bushes in which a pair builds its open cup-shaped nest from dry grasses and roots. Two eggs form the normal clutch and the incubation period lasts 14 days. Only the hen sits on the eggs. Cock and hen both feed the chicks until they fledge between three and four weeks of age.

The parents must be provided with plenty of insects, smooth caterpillars, spiders, flies and locusts. Soft fruit, sponge cake soaked in honey mixture, finely chopped figs and dates, raisins, currants and sultanas are enjoyed. Crumbled rusks may also be mixed with fruit. Grated carrot and soaked stale bread and milk may be given. Grit, ground egg shells and some greenfood should also be fed.

As soon as the young are able to feed themselves, they should be separated from their parents before any further breeding takes place, or they may be attacked. Cock birds assume full colour at about one year of age.

A Blue-Capped Tanager

111

EMERALD-SPOTTED TANAGER ◆

Tangara guttata
Origin: South America

An attractive, small tanager of slightly more delicate constitution than some of the larger types, it requires correct feeding and a high standard of cleanliness. It is not a difficult bird to keep, but extra care and attention is important.

Description:
Size: 13 cm (5 in)

COCK:

Body: bright green. Underparts: white with dark flecks. Head: spotted with black. Breast: green spotted with black. Beak: upper mandible, black; lower mandible, beige. Legs: grey.

HEN:

Similar, but lacks the yellow on forehead and around eyes. Sometimes a little larger than the cock. Colour of body more grey-green than the cock.

An Emerald-Spotted Tanager

Diet: (Softbill)
Apples, pears, sweet oranges and grapes form the basic diet. Sponge caked soaked in nectar mixture is enjoyed. Fine grade insectile mix should be used to coat diced fruit. Some livefood should be given including mealworms and well cleaned maggots.

Careful acclimatisation is needed and it is necessary to house this species inside during the winter months. Alternatively, it may be kept in a heated conservatory throughout the year. It should be sprayed regularly with a mist spray to keep plumage in good condition and free from food and droppings.

Breeding:
Breeding may be difficult, so encourage a pair by housing them in a well planted aviary with plants which are difficult to destroy, such as the tough-leaved Cheese Plant (*Monstera*). Both the cock and hen share in building the cup-shaped nest. A base may be provided in the form of canary nest pans or wicker baskets suspended from tall plants.

Two eggs are normally laid and the hen sits alone for the 14-day incubation period. The chicks are dependent on their parents for about three weeks. Try to offer plenty of livefood, such as mealworms, spiders, maggots and smooth caterpillars. Soft fruits and soaked dried fruit, such as currants, raisins, sultanas, figs and dates, are enjoyed and may be dusted with fine grade insectile mix. Fresh ants' eggs are eagerly accepted and greenfood should also be offered. The young should be separated from their parents as soon as they are seen to be feeding themselves, so that another round may be bred.

GREEN TWINSPOT ● ○ ■

Mandingoa nitidula
Origin: East Africa

This is not an easy bird to establish and its management is difficult for the inexperienced fancier. It is a rather delicate species, which always needs more care than most other types of seedeater. It is, however, a striking, attractive bird, which agrees well with most types of small waxbill, though breeding results are better, if a pair is housed alone.

A Green Twinspot

Description:

Size: 10 cm (4 in)

COCK:

Body: olive green. Breast and stomach: black with white spots. Facial mask: orange-red. Beak: black. Legs: cream.

HEN:

Similar to the cock, but its facial mask is golden beige.

Diet: (Seedeater)

Mixed millets form the staple diet. Millet sprays are enjoyed and livefood is also necessary. Mealworms and maggots may be fed, if available, and spiders and small smooth caterpillars are very popular with this species. Grit and cuttlefish bone must always be available.

Breeding:

The cock performs his courtship display on the ground dancing round the hen with a feather in his beak. The hen responds by wagging her tail from side to side.

A pair should be provided with globular, wicker baskets hung in a well planted aviary. During the breeding season this bird must have livefood and only rears young if plenty of insects are provided. The aviary should be well protected from inclement weather at all times.

An average clutch of eggs numbers three. The incubation period is 13 days and both parents take turns in sitting. Egg rearing food, soaked seed and soaked bread are useful for helping to feed the young. They fledge in around three weeks.

113

Peter's Twinspot

PETER'S TWINSPOT ● ○ ■
Hypargos niveoguttatus
Origin: East Africa

This attractive bird requires careful acclimatisation and it should always be considered rather delicate, even when firmly established. It must be protected from sudden changes in temperature. A large aviary is not necessary, but a sunny position is preferred. It is pleasant natured and is very placid with other seedeaters.

Description:
Size: 13 cm (5 in)
COCK:
Head: brownish-grey. Back: reddish-brown. Neck, sides of head and chin: bright red. Upperparts: black with white spots on flanks. Wings: dark brown. Tail: black and red. Beak: black. Legs: cream to grey.
HEN:
Much less red on head, generally paler coloured and with fewer white spots.

Diet: (Seedeater)
A varied diet is necessary. Mixed millets, plain canary seed, spray millet and some livefood, including chopped mealworms, fresh ants' eggs and a little greenfood, form the basic diet. Germinated seed and grass seed are relished. In cold weather and while breeding, stale white bread soaked in milk, egg food and a little cod liver oil help to keep this bird in good condition. Fruit is also enjoyed, particularly oranges. Grit and cuttlefish bone are essential.

Breeding:
The display of the cock bird prior to breeding is similar to that of the Green Twinspot. A pair usually constructs a nest in bushes a little off the ground. Box and dwarf conifers are favoured nesting sites. Nest boxes may be provided, although they make their own nests quite successfully using grasses and other material. A narrow entrance passage is constructed.

During the breeding season the cock chases other birds away from the nest site, but otherwise he is peaceful. The young hatch in 13 days and fledge in a further three weeks. The young should be fed chopped mealworms, egg food, soaked bread and germinated seed for quite some time. They should not be expected to thrive on hard seed alone for several months after leaving the nest.

A pair of Cordon Bleu

CORDON BLEU WAXBILL ● ○
Uraeginthus bengalus
Origin: Central Africa

This is a popular member of the waxbill family which lives for many years in an aviary after proper acclimatisation. It is highly recommended for the novice fancier. Several pairs of these birds can be kept in a collection of waxbills. The Cordon Bleu is not aggressive, even when breeding.

Description:
Size: 10 cm (4 in)
COCK:
Body: greyish-fawn. Undersides: blue. Head: blue. Cheeks: red crescent-shaped patches. Beak: pinky-grey. Legs: beige.
HEN:
Similar, but easy to sex since she lacks the red cheek patches.

Diet: (Seedeater)
Mixed millets and plain canary seed form the basic diet. Greenfood is always welcomed and millet sprays are enjoyed. Grit and cuttlefish bone must always be available.

While this bird becomes hardy outside, it suffers from sudden changes in temperature and from damp. In winter, try to house the Cordon Bleu in an indoor flight or in a cage in a moderately warm room.

Breeding:
The cock bird displays to the hen by means of an amusing dance, which he performs with a straw in his beak, and a pleasant song.

The Cordon Bleu is usually free breeding. A pair builds a nest in a bush using any material it can find. Some fanciers provide open-fronted nest boxes or globular wicker baskets, but this is not always necessary.

The hen weaves an intricate nest which is lined with soft grasses and feathers, some of which she plucks from the cock's breast. The hen lays a number of eggs, normally between four and seven. Both parents take turns in sitting for the incubation period of 14 days.

Small livefood is necessary to rear the chicks successfully, including ants' eggs and mealworms. Insectile mix, seeding grasses, and egg food are welcomed. The addition of sponge cake soaked in a honey and water mixture may also prove popular with the parents.

A pair of Cordon Bleu

A Golden-Breasted Waxbill

maggots, grit and cuttlefish bone should be provided.

Try to bring these birds indoors or provide a dry warm shelter away from any draughts in cold weather. This bird should not need heated accommodation unless unwell.

Breeding:
The Golden-Breasted Waxbill may be intolerant of other birds when nesting, both of its own kind and of other species. This should not normally amount to more than chasing other birds away from the nest site. It does not interfere with other birds that are nesting.

The cock's mating song, a rather monotonous chirping, can be heard from early in the morning until dusk. He performs a dainty courtship dance.

Globular wicker nest baskets and open-fronted nest boxes may be provided. A pair may also build their own nest using various materials, including hair, wool teasings and feathers. Plenty of plant cover is needed to encourage these birds to breed.

Three to five white eggs are laid which, if fertile, should hatch in 11 to 12 days. The hen may tend to lay eggs all year round, but often the eggs prove to be infertile. Both parents share in the incubation.

Breeding birds should be fed plenty of small, livefood, sprouted seeds, mashed hard boiled egg yolk, fresh ants' eggs and fine grade insectile mix.

The young fledge with yellowish-grey body colour, yellowish-red tail feathers and black beaks.

The Cordon Bleu has been known to breed with the similar Blue-Breasted Waxbill, the St. Helena Waxbill and even with Bengalese.

GOLDEN-BREASTED WAXBILL ●
Estrilda subflava
Origin: West Africa

A neat and lively, small waxbill, this bird can be kept with ease in a mixed collection of waxbills and small finches.

Description:
Size: 10 cm (5 in)
COCK:
Body: olive grey and dark yellow. Sides: grey with fine yellow wavy lines. Eyebrows: red stripe. Legs: cream.
HEN:
Similar, but paler underneath, slightly smaller and lacking red eyebrow stripes.

Diet: (Seedeater)
Mixed millets, plain canary seed, millet sprays and seeding grasses are enjoyed. Greenfood, a few mealworms or cleaned

RED-EARED WAXBILL ●
Estrilda troglodytes
Origin: Central Africa

A lively and tolerant waxbill, this bird is easy to keep in a mixed collection with other waxbills, Bengalese, Zebra Finches, small mannikins and silverbills.

Description:
Size: 10 cm (4 in)
COCK:
Body: pinkish-beige. Wings: light brown. Tail: light brown. Eye stripes: red. Beak: red. Legs: cream. The cock assumes a pink colour on the belly during the breeding season.

HEN:

Similar, rather difficult to sex by appearance. Observe behaviour and look for pink colour on belly of cock.

Diet: (Seedeater)

Mixed millets and plain canary seed form the basic diet. Millet sprays and seeding grasses are relished. Greenfood, grit and cuttlefish bone must always be available.

The Red-Eared Waxbill is quite hardy but should have a frost-proof shelter or room for winter. When moulting, this bird needs a little extra attention and warmth, plus a few drops of cod liver oil.

Breeding:

The Red-Eared Waxbill should be encouraged to nest when there are plentiful supplies of fresh ants' eggs available for chick rearing.

The cock dances around his hen with a blade of grass in his beak. He has a "chirrupy" mating song. The hen often replies with a soft, quiet, gurgling sound.

If breeding, this bird requires a secluded corner of the aviary as it is easily frightened off the nest. Nesting boxes should be provided. The nest is constructed with a narrow entrance passage and lined with hair and wool, which should be placed on bushes near the nest site for the bird to pick up. A choice of boxes fixed at varying heights encourages this bird to breed.

The hen lays between three and five white pointed eggs and the incubation period lasts between 11 and 22 days, both parents taking it in turn to sit on the eggs.

Fresh ants' eggs, egg food and soaked and germinated millet seed should be fed to the parent birds.

The chicks are ready to leave the nest 14 days after hatching. The fledglings are pale grey in colour with black beaks. A few weeks later they assume adult plumage.

This waxbill has on many occasions bred with the Orange-Cheeked Waxbill, Golden-Breasted Waxbill and the Crimson-Rumped Waxbill, producing attractive, unusually marked birds.

A Red-Eared Waxbill

ORANGE-CHEEKED WAXBILL ●

Estrilda melpoda
Origin: West Africa

This is an attractive member of the waxbill family. The many different species in this group all live together agreeably, although this one can be rather timid and shy on occasion. It is very hardy once acclimatised and has rather endearing habits, one of which is wagging its tail from side to side when excited or frightened.

Description:
Size: 10 cm (4 in)
COCK:
Body: fawnish-brown. Head, crown, chin and throat: pale grey. Rump: crimson. Tail: black. Cheek patches: bright orange. Beak: red. Legs: greyish-cream.
HEN:
Very similar, but orange cheek patches are a little smaller.

An Orange-Cheeked Waxbill

Diet: (Seedeater)
Mixed millets and plain canary seed, spray millet, seeding grasses and some greenfood keep this species in excellent health. Grit and cuttlefish bone must always be available.

Breeding:
Pairs are not always very successful in attempts at breeding. They sit rather fitfully, often leaving the eggs if disturbed, and fail to incubate them properly. Favoured nesting sites are boxes, baskets or thick bushes in which a domed nest is constructed. All disturbances should be kept to a mimimum to give these timid birds the confidence to carry on nest building, successful incubation and rearing.

Four eggs form the usual clutch and the incubation period is 11 days. Plenty of small livefood is necessary to help the parents feed their young. Aphids, if available, or fruit flies, small smooth caterpillars and fresh ants' eggs are valuable food supplies. Soaked and sprouted seed is also very beneficial.

VIOLET-EARED WAXBILL ● ○

Granatina granatinus
Origin: West and South Africa

This is a delicate bird which needs more careful attention than other waxbill species. Try to gain experience with other, more easily managed waxbill types before keeping the Violet-Eared Waxbill. Although its feathers are rather soft in texture, a bird in good condition exhibits well. Only one pair should be kept in a mixed collection, since the cock is aggressive with other cock birds of his own kind, although tolerant of other birds.

Description:
Size: 13 cm (5 in)
COCK:
Body: dark rich brown. Forehead and rump: deep violet blue. Underparts: chestnut. Cheeks: violet. Tail: black. Beak: red. Legs: black.
HEN:
Similar, but lighter on head, back and underparts. Cheeks: very pale violet, so this bird can be sexed fairly easily. Hens are often in short supply.

Diet: (Seedeater)

The Violet-Eared Waxbill must have a daily ration of insects, ants' eggs, grubs and mealworms. Mixed millets and plain canary seed, millet sprays and some greenfood should also be provided, and grit and cuttlefish bone must always be available. Try to provide as varied a diet as possible.

This species needs extra care in cold weather and sometimes a little extra warmth. It should be protected from sudden changes in temperature.

Breeding:

The cock bird has a very pleasant song reminiscent of the lark. The hen also sings, but very softly.

Breeding is difficult: a secluded spot in which to nest and a very varied diet are required. This is one of the few waxbills which must have insect food, even outside the breeding season. Greenfood, such as chickweed, dandelion and groundsel, is useful when breeding. Seeding grasses, mashed hard boiled egg, cheese, grits, charcoal, finely grated cuttlefish bone and well washed, finely ground egg shells are necessary too. Try to encourage this bird to take fine grade insectile mix, even if it refuses at first.

Three to four eggs are laid and incubation takes 12 to 14 days. The young fledge in three weeks resembling the hen in appearance. On maturity, at around three months of age, the sexes can be identified. Otherwise, nest building and preparation is the same as with other waxbills.

A Violet-Eared Waxbill

CEDAR WAXWING ◆ △
Bombycilla cedrorum
Origin: North America

This is an easy-to-manage softbill, although watch out for a tendency to gain weight. It needs a large aviary and a carefully regulated diet. The smooth, silky plumage of the Cedar Waxwing is one of its most notable features. It is placid in nature and thrives well in groups. Several pairs may be kept together, mixing well with each other and with other species of similar size. If tame and steady, this bird makes an excellent exhibition species.

Description:
Size: 15 cm (6 in)
COCK:
Head: pink-olive merging into grey-brown. Back and upper breast as head. Rump: grey. Tail: grey and edged with yellow. Eye stripe: wide black band. White streaks under eye. Wings: black with bright red flashes. Crest: pink-olive. Beak: black. Legs: black.

HEN:
Alike, so it cannot be sexed by appearance. Observe behaviour to identify a cock bird.

Diet: (Softbill)
Coarse grade insectile mix, soaked currants and sultanas, raisins and apples should be provided. It also enjoys berries.

Encourage exercise by siting food and drinking vessels some distance away from favourite perching spots, so that the bird has to fly to reach them.

Breeding:
It is considered quite difficult to breed these birds, so try to keep several pairs. The aviary needs to be well planted: bushy conifers with high-mounted, cup-shaped wicker baskets and open-topped nest boxes set in the thickest foliage, are useful to encourage nesting.

Successful hatching of chicks requires hard work by the owner, as the parents must have a plentiful supply of insects including gnats, flies and mosquitoes. Outside the breeding season, the Cedar Waxwing shows less interest in livefood.

A group of cedar Waxwings

120

NAPOLEON WEAVER   ◀ ◇
Euplectes afra afra
Origin: West Africa

A lively and active weaver, which can be aggressive during the breeding season and is best kept with other weavers, whydahs, Cut-Throat Finches or even budgerigars.

Description:
Size: 10 cm (4 in)
COCK (in nuptial plumage, during the breeding season):
Head: Thick yellow ruff. Back: yellow. Body: black and yellow. Wings: black and buff. Throat: yellow. Eyes: black. Beak: black. Legs: black.
HEN:
Alike, so it is not possible to sex bird by appearance, outside the breeding season when both the cock and hen are light greyish-brown in colour.

When buying any type of weaver, look for bright eyes, a clean vent and well shaped legs and feet. Scruffy feathers are not a sign of ill health in this species, as it is a soft feathered bird and plumage is easily damaged.

Diet: (Seedeater)
Mixed millets and plain canary seed form the basic diet. Greenfood, grit and cuttlefish bone should always be available.

This hardy species may winter outside during the day, but should be provided with a dry, frost-proof shelter or unheated room at night.

Breeding:
A nest is constructed in a nest box, which should be provided. The weaver also uses old nests, vacated by other weavers, fashioned to its own liking.

Three to four eggs form an average clutch and incubation takes 12 days. Both parents take turns to sit on the eggs by day and roost in the next box at night. Chicks fledge in three weeks.

This bird is interesting in appearance and behaviour during the breeding season when the cock's display is really amusing to watch. He puffs out his feathers to display his yellow ruff to best advantage.

A Napoleon Weaver

121

PARADISE WHYDAH ○ ■ ◀
Steganura paradisea
Origin: Central Africa

This is a graceful, beautiful, easily tamed member of the whydah family, peaceful and tolerant with even the smallest finches. However, the cock bird may become aggressive when breeding. As three or four hens should be placed with one cock to achieve satisfactory breeding, many fanciers prefer to keep one cock bird on its own in a mixed collection.

The Paradise Whydah is a hardy bird which needs only protection from frost and a little extra care when moulting.

Description:
Size: 51 cm (20 in)
COCK:
Body: black. Chest: chestnut and beige. Wings, tail, beak, legs: black. Legs: black.
HEN:
Buff, streaked with dark brown all over.

The cock bird in nuptial plumage attains two very long central tail feathers. These are lost outside of the breeding season, when the whole plumage changes colour to resemble the drab colour of the hen.

Diet: (Seedeater)
Mixed millets, spray millet, greenfood and a little apple form the basic diet. Grit and cuttlefish bone must always be provided.

The cock bird spends most of his time perched high on a branch taking care not to damage his long tail. He does not like descending to ground level to feed, as his long tail is unwieldy, so food should be positioned on a pedestal or stand, where he can feed without spoiling his plumage.

Breeding:
In their natural state, whydahs are parasitic breeders. The hen lays her eggs in the nest of a small finch, which hatches them and rears the young. Every whydah species chooses a certain type of finch for this purpose whose young resemble its own chicks in feather colour and reflecting papillae (luminous markings in the roof of the mouth). The Paradise Whydah hen usually lays her eggs in the nests of the Melba Finch (*Pytilia melba*).

In captivity the Paradise Whydah has been successfully bred, using the Fire Finch (*Lagonosticta senegala*) as host with Bengalese to hatch and rear the young. Chicks should be fed on hard boiled egg mashed with baby rusks and chopped mealworms.

YELLOW-BACKED WHYDAH ◀ ◇

Coliuspasser macrourus
Origin: West Africa

This whydah has a beautiful yellow back when in breeding plumage, which is very striking. It is lively, alert and unaggressive with birds of similar size and habits.

Description:
Size: 20 cm (8 in) in breeding plumage. 14 cm (6 in) at other times.
COCK:
Body: black with some brown edging on wings. Shoulders and mantle: bright yellow during breeding season. Beak: black. Legs: dark brown. When not breeding the cock moults to resemble the hen.
HEN:
Slightly smaller and dull brown. Chin and throat bear a yellowish tinge. Stomach: white with brown streaks.

Diet: (Seedeater)
Plain canary seed, mixed millets and seeding grasses form the basic diet. Live-food and spray millet are appreciated. Greenfood is consumed occasionally, but not every bird enjoys it. Grit and cuttlefish bone must always be available.

A roomy aviary should be provided with a dry shelter for roosting. This species often tries to roost outdoors so it must be encouraged inside if the weather is damp. Low temperatures are not harmful to this bird, but wet weather can cause illness.

Breeding:
This whydah is not a parasitic species, but is polygamous: breeding is encouraged if each cock bird has several hens. Unfortunately, it is not always easy to obtain hens.

The male builds the nest himself using dried grass and small roots. The hen lines the nest with any soft material she can find, including feathers. She continues lining the nest even after the eggs are laid. By the time the young are ready to leave the nest, it is usually a very solid structure.

After mating has taken place, the cock does not share in incubation and rearing. He can be quite spiteful, often chasing and annoying the hen. Usually three or four eggs are laid and incubation takes 13 days.

A Yellow-Backed Whydah

YELLOW SPARROW ◀ ◇

Auripasser luteus
Origin: East Africa

This hardy, brightly coloured bird is very easy to manage and feed. It may be kept outside all year round, but must not be mixed with small finches as it can be aggressive. It agrees well with Java Sparrows, mannikins and some of the smaller weavers.

Description: (Seedeater)
Size: 13 cm (5 in)
COCK:
Head: yellow. Back: chestnut. Wings: brown. Tail: brown. Stomach: yellow. Beak: cream, turns black during breeding season. Legs: brown.
HEN:
Head: buffish-brown. Mantle: buffish-brown. Stomach: buff and yellow. Beak: cream.

Above: a Yellow
Sparrow
Right: Black-Chinned
Yuhinas

BLACK-CHINNED YUHINA ◆
Yuhina nigrimentum
Origin: Himalayas

This attractive, small softbill has interesting habits. It is a lively, inquisitive bird that is very entertaining when it raises its small crest. It lives contentedly with sugarbirds and tanagers.

Description:
Size: 10 cm (4 in)
COCK:
Body: dark olive brown. Chest: grey-white. Stomach: buff. Crest and chin: black. Beak: brown and orange. Legs: brown.
HEN:
Identical so cannot be sexed by appearance. Observe behaviour to identify the cock bird. The cock is very aggressive in defence of his territory and often puts to flight birds twice his size.

Diet: (Seedeater)
Mixed millets and plain canary seed form the basic diet. Millet sprays and greenfood are enjoyed. It also appreciates some livefood, particularly small smooth caterpillars and mealworms. Grit and cuttlefish bone must always be provided.

Although a very active bird, it does spend a great deal of time out of sight in dense vegetation, if such cover is provided in the flight.

Breeding:
This is a difficult species to encourage to breed and plenty of cover is needed. Nest boxes and wicker nest baskets should be provided, sited low down in dense foliage to tempt pairs to start nest building. A large untidy nest is constructed, which is dome-shaped with a side entrance. Gorse bushes often prove popular sites. Pairs only go to nest if left strictly alone, so do not inspect the nest.

Three to four eggs form a normal clutch, which the hen incubates alone. The incubation period lasts around 16 days. Both parents share in rearing the young.

Plenty of insects are necessary when young are in the nest. These should include small smooth caterpillars, small beetles and mealworms. Greenfood and plentiful supplies of sprouted seeds must be available.

Diet: (Softbill)
Fruit, including pears, grapes and sweet oranges, forms the basis of the diet. It also enjoys sponge cake soaked in a honey and water mixture and small berries. Small live insects and fine grade insectile mixture should be provided.

The Yuhina needs careful acclimatisation. It should be housed in a planted garden aviary or conservatory and needs a dry, frost-proof shelter in damp and cold weather. It can withstand fairly low temperatures, but does not tolerate damp.

Breeding:
Yuhina pairs are not keen on breeding unless housed on their own. They build nests in shrubs or climbing plants, using fine grasses and roots.

Few eggs are laid, three being the maximum. Incubation takes around 16 days. Plenty of small live insects must be provided for rearing, including fruit flies, if available, aphis, blackfly and houseflies. Mealworms and maggots are too tough skinned for this bird, but may be eaten if finely chopped.

ZEBRA FINCH ● ○ ■
Poephila guttata
Origin: Australia

The Zebra Finch is an ideal species with which to begin bird keeping, easy to house, feed and manage. It is also very easy to breed.

There are several different forms of this domesticated species. The description below is for the original colour.

Description:
Size: 13 cm (5 in)
COCK:
Body: grey. Underparts: buff and white. Ear patches: bright chestnut. Flanks: chestnut, spotted with white. Throat: black and white barred. Beak: red. Legs: orange.
HEN:
Similar, minus throat markings, chest barring, lobe and flank markings. Beak: paler red than the cock bird.

Other colour forms available are fawn, white, isabel, pied, silver-winged, and albino.

All the above thrive well in any type of aviary accommodation.

Diet: (Seedeater)
Plain canary seed and mixed millets form the basic diet. Dry seed alone keeps this species in excellent health. Millet sprays should be given as a treat and greenfood may be provided. Grit and cuttlefish bone must always be available.

Breeding:
Zebra finches nest in boxes or wicker baskets, which should be well packed with nesting material by the owner. A small space should be left to allow the pair to finish off their nest. This prevents them from making "sandwich nests", when eggs are laid in an empty box or basket and then another nest is built on top of them.

Zebra finches are very inquisitive and often inspect other birds' nests. If they are intent on their own nesting, however, they are less inclined to make a nuisance of themselves in this way.

Zebra Finches lay many eggs and attempt to breed at any time of year. They should not be allowed to breed too frequently as the hens become exhausted. It is best to allow a pair to rear only two nests of chicks per season. Segregate cocks and hens to prevent overbreeding.

Six eggs form an average clutch and eggs are laid on consecutive days. The incubation period usually begins after the second or third egg. One or two chicks hatch a couple of days after the rest. Both parents share in incubating the eggs and feeding the chicks. Wholemeal bread and milk, soaked seed and canary rearing food should be provided.

Chicks leave the nest at about 20 days of age. Any young birds which are slow in learning to feed themselves should be encouraged with millet sprays, which they find easier to manage. The parents may often be seen feeding their young on the ground at this stage.

As soon as they are independent, young stock should be removed from their parents and the cocks segregated from the hens to prevent them from attempting to breed before they are fully developed.

A Zebra Finch

An Indian Zosterops

INDIAN ZOSTEROPS ● ◆
Zosterops palpebrosa
Origin: India

The Zosterops is a lively addition to a mixed collection which may include waxbills, silverbills and Spice Birds, or softbills, such as sugarbirds, yuhinas and small tanagers. This warbler-like bird readily becomes tame and is a good exhibition species.

Description:
Size: 10 cm (4 in)
COCK:
Body: green. Breast: grey-white. Belly: grey-white. Chin: yellow. Throat: yellow. Eye ring: white feathers. Beak: black. Legs: grey.
HEN:
Similar, but these birds may be sexed by the attractive song of the cock bird.

Diet: (Softbill)
The basic diet consists of fruit, especially pears, sweet oranges and grapes, fine grade insectile mix and sponge cake soaked in a honey and water mixture. Small livefood is necessary, including mealworms, cleaned maggots, spiders and flies. This bird also enjoys crumbled rusks with grated carrot and finely chopped dates. Nectar should be available in drinkers at all times.

The delicate appearance of this bird is deceptive since it is surprisingly hardy and, once acclimatised, can winter successfully outside, if there is access to a frost-proof shelter.

Breeding:
If conditions are right, Indian Zosterops make good parents. Since these birds are difficult to sex, try to keep several in the aviary and a pair should become evident.

Breeding may be encouraged with an artificial nest, placed in a nest box. This may be added to by the pair. Sometimes, they construct a nest using grasses, roots and wool. Three to four pale turquoise, narrow shaped eggs are laid. There are no flecks on the shells of these eggs.

Plenty of live insects are needed to rear a nest of chicks, including greenfly, blackfly and spiders. Nests are usually located high up in the aviary.

CHAPTER 8

UNUSUAL SPECIES FOR A MIXED COLLECTION

AFTER A FANCIER acquires a certain amount of experience in bird keeping, he or she may wish to consider a new challenge and keep unusual birds. Detailed below is a selection of such birds. These birds may only be kept with a very limited selection and number of companions. Some may only be kept with their own kind and others need a great deal of space and a lake or pond, because of their large size.

All these birds are more difficult to manage, feed and accommodate than those discussed in Chapter 7.

RED-BELLIED CONURE
Pyrrhura frontalis frontalis
Origin: South Eastern Brazil

This species of conure (the name most usually given to South and Central American parrakeets) is friendly and may be kept in a colony of its own kind. It is not noisy like the Aratinga varieties of conure. In a large aviary it can be bred in a colony, although better results are obtained when a pair is housed alone.

This attractive and often comical bird also makes an excellent show bird as it is normally very confident. Several other kinds of Pyrrhura Conures are also frequently available. This type is not destructive to woodwork or aviary netting.

Description:
Size: 23 cm (9 in)
COCK:
Body: dark green on upperparts, light green from lower breast to stomach. Head: crown, dark green; forehead, maroon. Ear coverts: pale buff-brown. Sides of neck, upper breast and throat bear scaly markings which vary in colour between olive yellow and whitish-yellow. Maroon patch on stomach. Eyes: black. Beak: black. Legs: black. Bare patch of white skin surrounds eyes.
HEN:
Similar. Conures are all difficult to sex, but usually the cock has a broader and flatter head, while the hen's is more conical. Watch to see if a pair feeds each other, as this usually indicates they are cock and hen.

Diet: (Seedeater)
Feed as varied a diet as possible, including sunflower seed, plain canary seed, millet (white), oats, buckwheat, niger seed and hemp (if available). Peanuts may also be enjoyed. Place seed in separate dishes to see which is preferred. Spray millet is also relished. Give a choice of fruit including grapes, apples, cherries, pomegranates, pears and oranges. Boiled sweetcorn (maize) is often very popular with this bird. A little honey may be added to drinkers to make a nectar mixture.

Once acclimatised this is a very hardy bird which may remain outside all year round. A selection of next boxes should be provided for roosting. A colony of conures often all try to roost in one box.

A Red-Bellied Conure in a show cage

127

Breeding:

The cock is often seen feeding the hen during the breeding season. Four to five eggs form a normal clutch. Allow pairs as much privacy as possible during breeding preparations and incubation, and do not attempt nest inspection unless essential. Young conures usually emerge from the nest for the first time at around 42 to 43 days after hatching.

When rearing young the parents should be provided with plenty of greenfood, soaked seed and soaked millet sprays. Seeding grasses, chickweed, young dandelion leaves and heads, lettuce, thistle, cabbage and brussel sprout tops are all excellent. Plenty of fruit should also be provided.

BLUE-CROWNED HANGING PARROT
Loriculus galgulus
Origin: Malay Peninsula, Singapore, Sumatra

This colourful, miniature parrot has very engaging ways. It is more dainty in appearance than most parrotlike birds. It is inoffensive with tanagers if the aviary is fairly large. The name originates from the habit of sleeping upside down with its feet locked around a perch as it slumbers. Active and lively, this species performs interesting acrobatics. It has a pleasant sounding call and chatters in the early morning and at dusk. It does not destroy vegetation even when breeding.

Description:
Size: 12 cm (4½ in)
COCK:
Body: rich green. Head: blue-crowned with bright red patch at throat. Shoulders: yellow. Rump: red.
HEN:
Similar, but no red or yellow on body. Often larger than the cock. Immature cock birds resemble hens. Older hens sometimes attain a few red feathers at the throat.

Diet:
This is a nectar and fruit eating parrot. It enjoys grapes, apples, oranges and bananas and eagerly takes sponge cake soaked in nectar mixture. It also eats a small amount of plain canary seed on occasions. Sultanas, currants and raisins are also enjoyed. Dishes of nectar should be provided.

Breeding:
Pairs can be encouraged to nest in budgerigar nest boxes or logs. Crumbled bark should be placed in the base. They like plenty of cover and a really densely planted aviary should be cultivated.

Three eggs form an average clutch and the incubation period is 21 days. Large amounts of fruit are taken when the young are being reared. Chicks take six to seven weeks to become independent.

Hanging parrots are usually attentive parents and try very hard when rearing their chicks.

RED-BILLED HORNBILL
Tokus erythrorhynchus rufirostris
Origin: Southern Africa

While the larger hornbills are only practical in a zoo or bird garden, this is one member of the African species which can be kept satisfactorily in the same aviary as large softbills. It is smaller in size and more docile in nature than its larger relatives. An immature Red-Billed Hornbill makes the most delightful pet being clumsy, comic and affectionate. It becomes very tame, especially if kept on its own without a partner.

A Blue-Crowned Hanging Parrot

A Red-Billed Hornbill

Description:
Size: 46 cm (18 in)
COCK:
Body: whitish-grey. Wings: black and white. Beak: red. Legs: grey. Long black eyelashes a prominent feature.
HEN:
Similar, but slightly smaller.

Diet: (Softbill)
The diet must include meat, frozen day-old chicks (well thawed) and mice. The quantity taken depends on the individual bird. One chick per day is usually sufficient. Locusts, if available, are also enjoyed. Coarse grade insectile mix and fruit should be fed (see Chapter 5).

When acclimatised, this bird lives healthily for many years and winters outdoors without any problems.

Breeding:
All hornbills share the same unusual nesting habit. The cock walls up the hen inside the selected nesting hole for the entire duration of the incubation period and the first 14 days of the chicks' development.

They normally nest in holes in trees but pairs may be provided with a barrel raised on stilts with an entrance hole near the top as a suitable nest site.

Pairs plaster the nest entrance hole with mud, their own faeces and rotting leaves. When the hen can just about squeeze into the entrance hole, she goes in and settles down to lay. Meanwhile, the cock carries on plastering until only a tiny slot remains open.

The cock feeds his hen for the six-week nesting period pushing food through the small slot. The hen normally lays between one to six eggs, with three to four round white eggs being the average number. The eggs take 28 to 30 days to hatch and then the hen has to stay in the nest for a further 14 days while the chicks develop. By the time they are half-grown at 14 days, the hen begins to chip away at the entrance hole with her large beak until she has created a hole large enough to make her exit. The chicks then use their own droppings to re-seal the entrance against predators. The hen is now free to help the cock bird bring food to feed the chicks until they become independent.

FISCHER'S LOVEBIRD
Agapornis fischeri
Origin: Northern Tanzania

This species of lovebird is the only one that may be kept in a colony of its own kind with a relative degree of safety. It is unwise to attempt to mix any other types of lovebird. The Fischers Lovebird is very popular since it is hardy, amusing and has a great deal of personality.

Description:
Size: 13 to 14 cm (5 to 6 in)
COCK:
Body: green. Forehead: bright red. Head, face, neck and breast: orange-red with olive green cast. Beak: red. Legs: grey.
HEN:
Alike. It is hard to sex this species, but sometimes the shape of the head varies between cock and hen. Observe behaviour, and look for one bird feeding another, which normally indicates a pair.

Diet: (Seedeater)
Plain canary seed and mixed millet form the basic diet. Provide a small quantity of sunflower seed and hemp seed. Grit and cuttlefish bone are essential.

This robust bird thrives outside all year round, but should have a dry shelter which is frost-, damp- and draught-proof.

Breeding:
A large aviary is desirable with plenty of budgerigar type nest boxes placed high up in the quarters, and well spaced to avoid quarrels. Provide branches for use as nesting material.

Soaked seed is useful for rearing, but pairs feed their young quite successfully on hard seed. Three or four eggs are laid and the incubation period is around 21 days. Both parents take turns in feeding the young and all parental duties. This species can be cross-bred with other lovebirds such as the Masked and the Peach-Faced Lovebird; in which case separate the pair to their own breeding quarters.

A pair of Fischer's Lovebirds

BLUE AND YELLOW MACAW

Ara ararauna
Origin: South America

This is a very spectacular, colourful bird which is very hardy and becomes extremely attached to its owner. Despite its hefty body and huge beak, it is a gentle natured bird. If kept alone, it is a very tame and talented talking pet and, if provided with a compatible mate and suitable conditions, usually attempts to breed.

It is quite feasible to keep several different macaws together in a large, outdoor aviary, preferably sited in a large garden well away from neighbours. The aviary should be constructed of chain link, since the macaw''s heavy beak destroys anything less robust. If kept at liberty, the Macaw must be trained. First, clip its wings. Then house the bird in a barrel in a tree, cut out the front of the barrel and replace with wire mesh. Place the food supply inside the barrel. After a few days, allow the bird to emerge to investigate its surroundings and climb about in its tree. It soon learns to return to the barrel to roost. By the time its wings have grown again, the bird is trained.

Description:
Size: 86 cm (34 in)
COCK:
Chest: yellow. Wings: blue. Tail: blue and yellow. Under tail coverts: greenish-blue. Bare skin on face: greyish-white with tiny black feathers. Black band around neck and throat. Eyes: pale yellow. Beak: black. Legs: dark grey.
HEN:
Similar, but slightly smaller with a smaller beak.

Diet: (Seedeater)
Sunflower seed, peanuts, soaked maize, dry biscuits and rusks, all kinds of fruit and greenfood should be provided. Boiled rice may be given and fresh twigs are appreciated. Grit and cuttlefish bone should always be available.

Breeding:
A barrel should be provided for breeding pairs. It requires a large hole cutting in the front near the top. A thick layer of sawdust should be placed in the base. The hen lays no more than two or three eggs and the incubation period is 25 days. Young macaws do not emerge from the nest until three months of age. It takes six months before they attain full adult colouration.

Several other large macaws may be kept at liberty or in a large aviary. These include the:

Scarlet Macaw (*Ara macao*)
Military Macaw (*Ara militaris militaris*)
Green-Winged Macaw (*Ara chloroptera*)
Hyacinthine Macaw (*Anodororhynchus hyacinthinus*).

A pair of Blue and Yellow Macaws

LESSER HILL MYNAH
Gracula religiosa indica
Origin: India

This bird is an engaging comic and becomes very tame. It has a keen talent for mimicry. It should not be kept with birds that are breeding, because it may steal and eat their young. It can be accommodated with other species over 25 cm (10 in) in size which are not breeding.

A further species, the Greater Hill Mynah (*Gracula r religiosa*) from Indonesia is slightly larger, up to 33 cm (13 in), and is also frequently available. It requires the same feeding and management as the Lesser Hill Mynah.

Description:
Size: 25 cm (10 in)
COCK:
Body: black. Cere: yellow. Crown: yellow.
Eye patch: bare yellow skin. Beak: orange-yellow. Legs: yellow.
HEN:
Alike. Cannot be sexed by appearance, so observe behaviour.

Diet: (Softbill)
Insectile mixture in coarse grade quality should be provided mixed with raw meat or mealworms. All kinds of fruit are accepted as are table scraps such as boiled vegetables and meat. Dry boiled rice mixed with hard boiled egg can also be fed.

It must be protected against frost and should ideally be housed indoors in cold weather. The droppings are very messy, so it is better kept in an aviary than a cage.

Breeding:
This species is difficult to encourage to breed. A pair may attempt to nest in a hollow log or small barrel. Plenty of live food is necessary if young are produced.

A Lesser Hill Mynah

INDIAN RING-NECKED PARRAKEET
Psittacula Krameri manillensis
Origin: India and Sri Lanka

This parrakeet may sometimes be kept with other large birds, but certain individuals are more aggressive than others and so great care must be exercised. A breeding pair must always be housed alone.

This smooth feathered parrakeet can also be obtained in a superb lutino (yellow) form and a blue mutation. It often makes a winning show bird, as its plumage looks so immaculate.

Description:
Size: 40 cm (15 in)
COCK (normal green type):
Body: mainly green with yellow underparts. Chin: black with a black band beneath the beak. Neck: bears a rose-pink collar. Nape of neck: blue. Wings: green with some dark blue and a little red. Beak: rose-pink.
HEN:
Lacks the collar and black band. An immature cock resembles a hen.

Diet: (Seedeater)
Sunflower seed, plain canary seed, mixed millets and oats form the basic diet. Apple and other fruit is enjoyed. Grit and cuttlefish bone must always be available.

This hardy bird may be kept outside all year round, but should be provided with a frost-proof shelter, as it is prone to frost-bitten toes. It is a strong flyer and needs a fairly large aviary to exercise its wings.

Breeding:
A large nest box should be placed fairly high up in the aviary or shelter. The base should be filled with sawdust, wood shavings and some rotton wood. The cock whistles softly while the hen adjusts the nest to her liking. These preparations are quite interesting to observe. The birds seem very cheerful at this time. Three to four eggs are laid and the hen incubates alone. Both cock and hen feed the chicks and are eager to take germinated seeds, fruit, some hard seeds, rusks soaked in milk and some fresh ants' eggs, if available.

CHUKOR PARTRIDGE
Alectoris graeca chukor
Origin: India and Himalayas

This interesting bird requires a large aviary with a rockery, since it needs large stones and boulders to feel comfortable. The Chukor Partridge, especially the hen, becomes very tame. Only one pair can be kept in a well planted aviary, or even in a garden, if one wing is pinioned permanently. Do not keep more than one hen to a cock, or he is likely to kill the spare hen or hens. This bird must not be kept with other ground birds, but may safely be associated with large perching birds. It can remain outside all year round.

Above left: an Indian Ring-Necked Parrakeet

Below: a pair of Chukor Partridges in a suitable nest site

133

Description:

Size: 36 cm (14 in)

COCK:

Body: grey-beige. Throat: yellowish-white with a black band. Sides: black stripes on a brownish-yellow ground. Legs: red with small spurs. Eye ring: red. Beak: red.

HEN:

Smaller than the cock and normally lacks spurs, but some hens develop small spurs in old age.

Diet: (Seedeater)

Mixed millets, maw seed and finely chopped greenfood, such as lettuce and chickweed, form the basic diet. Egg food should be fed to breeding pairs. Some grit should be provided.

Breeding:

The cock bird pursues the hen ardently during the breeding season. Eight to twelve eggs form an average clutch, and are laid in depressions between stones or in small holes. If the hen shows a reluctance to incubate the eggs, they may be placed under a Bantam hen or in an incubator.

The young appear after 24 days. Feed them on plenty of chopped greenfood, maw seed and egg food, adding millet seed as they grow. Youngsters attain adult plumage at three months of age and their beak turns from black to red. At eight months of age the cock starts to show his spurs.

This is an unusual bird with interesting habits. It can reproduce large numbers each season, if the eggs are removed from the hen each day as soon as they are laid, and incubated elsewhere. As many as 40 chicks can be reared in this manner.

An Indian Peacock: "the bird of a thousand eyes"

INDIAN PEAFOWL
Parvo cristatus
Origin: India

The striking peacock is so well known, a description is hardly necessary. It is often known as "the bird of a thousand eyes", due to the eye-like markings on its feathers. Despite its size and magnificence, the peafowl is not an expensive bird to purchase. It has a piercing cry early in the morning and at dusk so do not purchase this species, unless you have plenty of space available and tolerant, deaf or distant neighbours. This species particularly enjoys the company of domestic fowl.

Description:

Size: 122 cm (48 in)

COCK:

Body: greenish-turquoise. Distinctive eye-like markings on wings. Crest: greenish-blue. Legs: black. Eyes: black. Body: dappled with black/brown. Train: may comprise up to 150 feathers.

HEN:

Varying shades of brown and beige with black markings.

Diet:

Turkey pellets, wheat and greenfood form the basic diet. It forages for insects, if kept in a large garden or a parkland setting. In a wired-in enclosure, the owner needs to supply livefood.

This bird must be given plenty of space so that it does not damage its fine plumage. A number of different varieties may be obtained including a pied and an all white form. The most elegant feature of the cock bird is his magnificent train. In display the wings are fanned to show the eye-like markings in all their glory.

Breeding:

The cock bird may have up to five or six hens if permitted. Though a polygamous bird, one hen is usually sufficient.

The hen nests just off the ground in thick grass and shrubs and lays between four and eight eggs. The incubation period is around 27 to 30 days, with 28 being the most usual. Peahens are very protective mothers. The chicks develop quite slowly and take three months to become independent.

SILVER PHEASANT
Lophura n. nycthemera
Origin: South China

A large, interesting member of the pheasant family, closely related to domestic poultry with whom it mixes amicably. The brilliant white of its plumage is eye catching. There are many sub-species of Silver Pheasant, all most attractive.

It may be allowed freedom, if a wing is clipped to prevent it flying away. This has to be repeated after each moult when the feathers grow again, or may be done permanently while the bird is young. This species is much quieter than other pheasants.

Description:
Size: 86 cm (34 in)
COCK:
Body: chalky white with wavy black lines. Chin: black. Throat: black. Crest: black. Assumes full colour at two years of age.
HEN:
Body: olive brown with black markings. Chin: grey spots. Throat: grey spots. Chest: edged with black.

Diet:
The basic diet consists of mash and chicken feed, with chick rearing grain added when breeding. Proprietary brands of this feed may be purchased. It may share the same feed as poultry. This pheasant also appreciates greenfood, such as grass, lettuce and chickweed. Proprietary brand pheasant pellets are also available from pet food suppliers. Oats, hemp (if available) and maize should be added in cold weather.

This pheasant is placid and may also be housed with budgerigars and some of the larger parrakeets. It should not be kept with breeding finches, as it eats the young birds as soon as they leave the nest. It can be kept with finches that are not breeding, however.

Since the Silver Pheasant spends most of its time on the ground, it only requires a couple of sturdy perching branches which should be located in the shelter to ensure it roosts in a dry spot.

This bird likes to spend a great deal of time pacing around the perimeter of its quarters and, for this reason, the area may be concreted and sprinkled with fine

A Silver Pheasant

gravel, which is easier to keep clean than a soil base. Hay or straw should be provided in the shelter in cold weather to protect the bird from frost-bitten toes and legs. In hot weather it is advisable to cover the shelter floor with peat, if it is made of concrete.

The Silver Pheasant flies upwards suddenly when alarmed, so it is worthwhile using nylon netting for the top of the aviary rather than wire mesh. This should only be used if the bird is housed with poultry, since budgerigars and parrakeets would escape through such a covering.

Breeding:
Pheasants are not easy birds to breed. Very few raise their own young and most fanciers use Bantam hens to foster pheasant chicks. Pheasant hens lay in their first year, but these eggs usually prove infertile. In the second year they can lay up to 16 eggs. The incubation period lasts 25 to 27 days. Be very careful when entering the aviary, as the cock bird becomes aggressive when the hen is laying and may attack the owner.

In common with many other pheasants, two or three hens may be kept with one cock bird. In practice, a pair is probably enough to manage.

BLEEDING-HEART PIGEON
Gallicolumba luzonica
Origin: The Philippines

A striking member of the pigeon family, which gains its name from the bright red spot in the centre of its breast. Easy to manage, this species may be kept singly or in a pair in a mixed collection with other large birds, but often disagrees with others of its own kind.

Description:
Size: 25 cm (10 in)
COCK:
Head: pale grey. Body: dark grey. Cheeks: white. Breast: red and white. Throat: white. Belly: yellowish-white. Wings: grey with brown and black bands. Eyes: dark brown. Legs: maroon red.

A Bleeding-Heart Pigeon

HEN:
Similar, but red on the breast is much smaller. Lower parts: buff.

Diet: (Seedeater)
The basic diet consists of mixed millets, plain canary seed, oats, hemp and wheat. Mealworms are accepted and the bird actively forages on the ground for insects, worms and snails. It also enjoys stale white bread crumbled into a mix with grated carrot. Cod liver oil should be added to its seed mix occasionally to maintain good health. Grit and cuttlefish bone must be provided.

The Bleeding-Heart Pigeon is hardy and may winter outside if it has access to a dry, frost-proof shelter for roosting.

Breeding:
This pigeon requires some thick shrubbery in which to construct a nest for breeding. The aviary should be well planted to give plenty of cover. It is best to prepare a wire mesh support for the nest, which should be located at a fairly low level.

Straw and grasses and some twigs should be made available for pairs. They are not expert nest builders. The cock bird fetches and carries materials for the hen to fashion into a rather messy and untidy nest.

Once she has completed her preparations, the hen lays two eggs. The incubation period lasts 14 days and during this time both parents sit on the eggs, the cock taking his turn during the day. The cock bird feeds the hen all the time she is on the nest.

This species is rather prone to cases of dead-in-shell and infertile eggs (see page 37). If all is well, the young emerge from the nest in ten days. When rearing their young, the parents need additions to their diet, such as fresh ants' eggs and egg rearing food. Plenty of extra livefood is necessary and mealworms are eagerly taken.

The youngsters are very shy when they first leave the nest. They do not gain any signs of the red breast until they are six to seven weeks of age. They are fully developed at 16 weeks.

Cock and hen should be separated during winter months or the hen becomes weak from too frequent attempts at breeding.

TOCO TOUCAN
Ramphastos toco
Origin: Central and South America

This bird is best kept alone or with a mate, providing the pair is compatible. Toucans are not good at living with other birds, particularly with other toucans, and even true pairs have been known to fight. Some fanciers, however, have been successful in keeping them with birds such as jays.

A single Toco Toucan makes a most rewarding pet and becomes very tame with its owner. It can be taught to catch grapes with the tip of its huge beak and it tosses them down its throat with an amusing action. The huge beak is cellular, almost hollow and very light. It is far more delicate than one would think and can be damaged quite easily.

Description:
Size: 51 to 56 cm (20 to 22 in)
COCK:
Body: black. Rump: white. Cheeks: white. Throat and breast: white, tinged with orange. Tail coverts: red underneath. Beak: orange-red with black bands. Eye patch: orange. Eyes: blue. Legs: blue-grey.
HEN:
Similar, but beak shorter and deeper with a blunter tip.

Diet: (Softbill)
The diet comprises fruit of all kinds, orange, apple, pear, grape and banana. It should be diced into cubes the same size as sugar lumps. Coarse grade insectile mix should be given and some raw meat. If the bird shows a reluctance to take a particular item, all the ingredients should be mixed together to form pellets. Soaked raisins, currants, sultanas, dates and dried figs are enjoyed. If possible, a small dead mouse, or a frozen chick, which may be purchased from pet food suppliers, should be provided on occasionally.

Since the Toco Toucan destroys plants, it is pointless to providing a planted aviary. A tall flight is needed since it prefers to perch high. It leaps in great bounds from branch to branch and must be provided with strong branches to bear its weight. It needs a little extra warmth in winter.

Breeding:
Breeding successes in captivity are rarely reported. However, to encourage a pair to attempt to nest, a barrel or tree trunk with a hole should be provided.

A Toco Toucan

WHITE-CRESTED TOURACO

Tauraco leucotis
Origin: Africa

A handsome species and fine exhibition bird with a very shiny plumage, the White-Crested Touraco is often called a "Go-Away Bird", due to its call which sounds as though it is saying this. The only drawback is the loud raucous tone of its voice. It is a very agile tree climber with a liking for sitting high up in branches. It may be kept with birds of similar size and habits, including large pigeons.

Description:
Size: 41 cm (16 in)
COCK:

Head: black and white. Crest: white. Eye ring: red. Breast: green. Chest: violet-blue. Feet: four toes, two in front and two behind. Tail: Long and square.

A White-Crested Touraco

HEN:
Alike, but not so large and has a shorter tail.

Diet: (Softbill)
This species needs plenty of fruit, boiled rice and boiled potatoes, which can also be mixed with boiled carrots. Many kinds of greenfood are enjoyed. Live insects should be fed.

This bird requires a large aviary and needs a little heat in winter if the weather is severe. It is hardy once established and lives for many years.

Breeding:
Pairs are a little difficult to encourage to breed. Nests are constructed in trees with plenty of twigs. A small clutch of three eggs is normal. The incubation period is 18 days and the young fledge in around four weeks. Young touracos can climb about very easily and speedily, long before they learn to fly. They are aided by a special claw on their wing.

WATERFOWL
A brief note

Those fanciers who have large ground areas to spare, with a small lake or pond, may like to keep some waterfowl.

Geese, swans or ducks are not difficult to keep providing correct attention is paid to their diet.

Diet:
The standard diet should consist of mixed grains, such as wheat, maize and barley. Peas, beans and lettuce should also be fed. Do not offer cabbage to a duck however as it is too tough and leathery to digest. Certain proprietary brands of dog feed mixtures can also be offered.

Troughs should be provided to contain the feed for these species. They should be located well away from water to avoid the food becoming messy and unhygienic. Uneaten food should not be left in troughs, as it encourages vermin.

A group of ducks beside a small lake

GLOSSARY

Aviary	Accommodation for keeping birds either in or out of doors.
Aviculture	Keeping of birds in captivity.
Bobhole	Entry hole in shelter.
Brood	Group of chicks in the nest.
Cere	Small patch devoid of feathers above the beak of certain birds, e.g. budgerigars.
Chick	Infant bird.
Clear Egg	Infertile egg.
Closed Ring	Aluminium closed ring for fitting on leg of chick to prove it is owner bred and to record its age.
Clutch	Eggs laid by a hen in one sitting.
Cock	Male bird.
Coverts	Feathers above the secondaries on the wings and those above the long tail feathers.
Crop	Area of the throat where food is ground up with grit the bird has swallowed.
Dead-in-shell	Chicks that do not develop properly and die before hatching.
Domesticated	Species that has been consistently bred in captivity for many generations.
Down	Fluffy layer beneath quills.
Egg Binding	Hen's inability to lay an egg.
Fancier	Person who enjoys the hobby of bird keeping.
Feather Plucking	Removal of feathers by a bird, either its own or those of companions.
Fledgling	A young bird emerging from the nest for the first time.
Flight	Exercise area for birds usually constructed with wire netting or mesh.

French Moult	Disease causing unnatural loss of wing and tail feathers, most often experienced when breeding budgerigars.
Hand Rearing	Rearing of chicks performed by fancier if birds refuse to feed their young.
Hen	Female bird.
Hybrid	Result of crossing two different species, or of well marked varieties within a species.
Incubation	Period of time after the last egg is laid until the chicks hatch.
Juvenile Moult	First moult of young birds.
Moult	Feathers drop out and are replaced by new ones.
Mule	Result of crossing a canary with a British finch.
Mutation	Chromosomal change or colour or character.
Nuptial Plumage	Unusual colour of long feathers sported by cock birds only during the breeding season.
Pair Bonding	Cock and hen choose each other as mates, often for life.
Pied	Bird whose colour is interspersed with light areas.
Pin Feather	Feather still encased in its sheath.
Plumage	Collective term used to describe both quill feathers and down.
Preening	Grooming of feathers by birds to distribute oil from the gland at base of tail. Birds also preen each other.
Quill	Main shaft of a feather.
Seedeater	Bird which lives on a diet of seed.
Shelter	Enclosed part of aviary for roosting.
Softbill	Bird which lives on a diet of fruit, insects, nectar, meat or multi-ingredient insectile mixtures, or a combination of these.
Split Rings	Coloured plastic rings which may be fitted on the leg of a bird of any age for identification.
Steady	Term for a confident and calm bird.
Vent	Anus.

INDEX

Abscess 35
Accommodation 7
African Silverbill 104, (105)
Ailments 35
American Holly 16
Andaman Mynah 88
Ants' Eggs 23
Asian Fairy Bluebird 72
Aspergillosis 35
Asthma 35
Avadavat, Red 55
Aviary – construction 8
       – drainage 8
       – entrance 7
       – flooring 9
       – indoor 12
       – location 7
       – outdoor 7
       – protection 9
       – ventilation 10
Avocet 48

Bacterial infection 36
Bark 24
Barley 23
Baths and pools 20
Bengalese 56
Berberis 15
Bengalese as foster parents 33
Bicheno 57
Bird bath 20
Bird ringing 31
Blackberry 15
Black-Chinned Yuhina 124
Black-Crested Bulbul 60
Black-Headed Mannikin 84, (86)
Bleeding 36
Bleeding-Heart Pigeon 136
Blue and Yellow Macaw 131
Blue-Capped Tanager 111
Blue-Crowned Hanging Parrot 128
Bob hole 11
Border Fancy Canary 61
Botulism 38
Bourke's Parrakeet 91
Box hedging 16
Boxes and baskets 28
Bread and milk 31
Breeding 27
Broken bones 36
Buckwheat 23
Budgerigar 58, 59
Bulbul, Black-Crested 60
Bumblefoot 36

California Quail 100
Camera equipment 44
Canary, Border Fancy 61
Canary rearing food 23
Canary seed 23
Cancer 23
Cardinal, Green 62
Cardinal, Pope 63
Cardinal, Red-Crested 64
California Quail 100
Carnivorous 26

Cataract 36
Catching net 21
Cattle Egret (47)
Cedar Waxwing 120
Charcoal 23
Chestnut-Breasted Finch 65
Chicken egg shells 23
Chickweed 23
Chinese Painted Quail 101
Chukor Partridge 133
Clear eggs 29
Closed metal rings 31, (42)
Clover 23
Clutch 34
Coccidiosis 36
Cockatiel 66
Cockatoo 48
Cod liver oil 23
Cold 36
Colour slides 45
Common Elderberry 16
Conifer – Little Gem 16
        – Nana 16
Conjunctivitis 37
Constipation 37
Conure, Red-Bellied 127
Cordon Bleu Waxbill 115
Cotoneaster 16
Courtship 27
Crickets 26
Crop impaction 37
Currants 25
Cut-Throat Finch 67
Cuttlefish bone 23
Cyst 37

Dandelion 23
Dead-in-shell 37
Diamond Dove 70
Diamond Sparrow 68, 69
Diarrhoea 37
Diet – Seedeater 22
     – Softbill 24
Display 41
Dove Diamond 70
Dove Laughing 70, (71)
Drinking tube (20)

Eagle Owl (47)
Eclectus Hen 48
Egg binding 37
Egg laying 27
Egg sac rupture 37
Egret, Cattle (47)
Elderberry – Common 16
           – European 16
           – Red 16
Elegant Grass Parrakeet 92
Emerald-Spotted Tanager 112
English Holly 16
English Ivy 16
Enteritis 37
Equipment 19
European Elderberry 16
Exhibiting 41

Fairy Bluebird, Asian 72
Feather mites 38
Feather plucking 38

Feeding 22
Feeding dishes 19
Finch – Bengalese 56
      – Bicheno 57
      – Chestnut-Breasted 65
      – Cut-Throat 67
      – Gold 74
      – Gouldian 75
      – Green Singing 78, 79
      – Lavender 84, (85)
      – Parson 98
      – Spice 104, (106)
      – Star 106, (107)
      – Zebra 125
Fire Finch, Vinaceous 73
First aid box 21
Fischer's Lovebird 130
Fits 38
Flamingo 48
Fledging 28
Flight 7
Forsythia 17
Fostering with Bengalese 33
French moult 38
Frugivorous 26
Fruit Fly larvae 25
Fruitsucker, Golden-Fronted 73

Gannet (46)
Germinating seed 22
Going light 38
Goitre 38
Golden-Breasted Waxbill 116
Golden-Fronted Fruitsucker 73
Goldfinch 74
Gouldian Finch 75
Gout 38
Grass Parrakeet, Elegant 92
Grass Parrakeet, Splendid 95
Grass Parrakeet, Turquoisine 95, (96)
Grassfinch, Heck's 76
Grassfinch, Long-Tailed 76
Grassfinch, Masked 77, (78)
Green Cardinal 62
Green Singing Finch 78, (79)
Green Twinspot 112, (113)
Greenfood 23
Grit 23
Groats 23
Ground birds 23
Groundsel 23

Hand rearing 29
Hanging Parrot, Blue-Crowned 128
Hard boiled egg 23
Harmful plants 15
Hatching 28
Hawfinch, Japanese 80
Hawthorn 17
Heart disease 38
Heck's Grassfinch 76
Hemp seed 23
Hill Mynah, Lesser 132
Hill Toucan, Laminated (49)
Holly – English 16
      – American 16
Honey 22
Honeysuckle 17
Hopper, seed 20

Hornbill, Red-Billed 128, (129)
Hospital cage 21
Hydrogen Peroxide 36
Hygiene 24

Incubation 27
Incubator 21
Indian Blue Roller 103
Indian Peafowl 134
Indian Ring-Necked Parrakeet 133
Indian Zosterops 126
Infertile eggs 29
Insectile mixture 24
Insectivorous 26
Ivy, English 16
Ixulus, Yellow-Collared 81

Japanese Hawfinch 80
Java Sparrow 81, (82)
Jay, Pileated 82, (83)
Juniper, Blue Star 17
Juvenile moult 28

King Vulture (47)

Laburnum 24
Laminated Hill Toucan (49)
Laughing Dove 70, (71)
Laughing Thrush, White-Crested 83
Laurel 24
Lavender Finch 84, (85)
Lesser Hill Mynah 132
Lice 38
Limberneck 38
Liquid multi-vitamins 23
Locusts 26
Long-Tailed Grassfinch 76
Lovebird, Fischer's 130
Lutino Cockatiel (66)

Macaw, Blue and Yellow 131
Maggots 25
Magpie Mannikin 86
Maize 23
Mange mites 39
Mannikin, Black-Headed 84, (86)
Mannikin, Magpie 86
Mannikin, White-Headed 87
Masked Grassfinch 77, (78)
Mating 27
Maw seed 22
Mealworms 25
Mice, protection from 9
Millet seed 22
Mites – Feather 38
       – Mange 39
       – Quill 38
       – Red 13
Mock Orange Blossom 17
Moorhen (45)
Moult 39
Mynah, Andaman 88
Mynah, Lesser Hill 132
Mynah, Pagoda 88, (89)
Mynah, Rothschild's 90
Mynah pellets 25
Mule 62

Napoleon Weaver 121

Nectar mixture 24
Nectivorous 26
Nephritis 39
Nest inspection 29
Nest sites 21, 27
Nutrition 22

Oats 23
Omnivorous 25
Orange-Cheeked Waxbill 118
Ornaments 21
Ornithosis 39
Overgrown beak and toe nails 39
Owl, Eagle (47)
Oyster Catcher (49)

Pagoda Mynah 88, (89)
Pair bonding 108
Paradise Whydah 122
Parrakeet, Bourke's 91
Parrakeet, Elegant Grass 92
Parrakeet, Indian Ring-Necked 133
Parrakeet, Plum-Headed 93
Parrakeet, Red-Rumped 93, (94)
Parrakeet, Sierra (43)
Parrakeet, Splendid Grass 95
Parrakeet, Turquoisine Grass 95, (96)
Parrot Finch, Pin-Tailed 96, (97)
Parson Finch 98
Partridge, Chukor 133
Peafowl, Indian 134
Peanut butter 25
Peanuts 23
Pekin Robin 99
Pelican (46)
Perches 19
Peter's Twinspot 114
Pheasant, Silver 135
Photographing birds 41, 44
Pigeon, Bleeding-Heart 135
Pigeon, Victoria Crowned (14)
Pileated Jay 82, (83)
Pin-Tailed Parrot Finch 96, (97)
Plantain 23
Plants 15
Plum-Headed Parrakeet 93
Pneumonia 39
Pope Cardinal 63
Preening 13
Psittacosis 39
Purple Sugarbird 109

Quail, California 100
Quail, Chinese Painted 101
Quelea, Red-Billed 102
Quill mites 38

Raisins 25
Raspberry 17
Raw meat 25
Rearing 29
Red Avadavat 55
Red-Bellied Conure 127
Red-Billed Hornbill 128, (129)
Red-Billed Quelea 102
Red-Crested Cardinal 64
Red-Eared Waxbill 116, (117)
Red Elderberry 16
Red mites 39

Red-Rumped Parrakeet 93, (94)
Regurgitation 39
Rheumatism 40
Rhododendron 15
Rickets 40
Ring-Necked Parrakeet, Indian 133
Rings, closed metal 31, (42)
Rings, split plastic 31
Robin, Pekin 99
Roller, Indian Blue 103
Roosting 50
Rose hip syrup 24
Rose, Wild 18
Rothschild's Mynah 90
Russian Vine 17

Safety door 21
Salmonellosis 40
Scaly face and leg 40
Seed hopper 20
Seeding grasses 23
Selecting birds 50
Selection of compatible birds 50
Shelter 7
Shepherd's Purse 23
Shock 40
Show 41
Show cage 41
Sierra Parrakeet (43)
Silver Pheasant 135
Silverbill, African 104, (105)
Sinus disorder 40
Snowberry 18
Snowy Owl (48)
Soaked seed 22
Sour crop 40
Sparrow, Diamond 68, 69
Sparrow, Java 81, 82
Sparrow, Yellow 123 (124)
Special Award 43
Spice Bird 104, (106)
Spiders 26
Spinach 23
Splendid Grass Parrakeet 95
Split plastic rings 31
Sponge cake 24
Sprouted seed 22
Star Finch 106, (107)
Starling, Superb Spreo 108
Stilt 48
Sugarbird, Purple 109
Sugarbird, Yellow-Winged 110
Sultanas 25
Sunflower seed 23
Superb Spreo Starling 108
Sweetcorn 23
Swollen oil gland 40

Tanager, Blue-Capped 111
Tanager, Emerald-Spotted 112
Thistle 23
Toco Toucan 136, (137)
Toucan, Laminated Hill (49)
Toucan, Toco 136, (137)
Touraco, White-Crested 138
Tumour 35
Turquoisine Grass Parrakeet 95, (96)
Twinspot, Green 112, (113)
Twinspot, Peter's 114

Vermin, protection from 9
Victoria Crowned Pigeon (14)
Vinaceous Fire Finch 73
Vine, Russian 17
Violet-Eared Waxbill 118, (119)
Vitamins 22
Vulture, King (47)

Waterfall (20)
Waterfowl 139
Waxbill, Cordon Bleu 115
Waxbill, Golden-Breasted 116
Waxbill, Orange-Cheeked 118
Waxbill, Red-Eared 116, (117)
Waxbill, Violet-Eared 118, (119)
Waxwing, Cedar 120
Weaver, Napoleon 121
Weaver, Red-Billed Quelea 102
Weeping Willow 18
Wheat 23
White-Crested Laughing Thrush 83
White-Crested Touraco 138
White-Headed Mannikin 87
White Java Sparrow 81
Whydah, Paradise 122
Whydah, Yellow-Backed 123
Wild Rose 18
Wired-in safety door 21
Worms 40

Yellow-Backed Whydah 123
Yellow-Collared Ixulus 81
Yellow Sparrow 123 (124)
Yellow-Winged Sugarbird 110
Yuhina, Black-Chinned 124

Zebra Finch 125
Zosterops, Indian 126

INDEX OF SCIENTIFIC NAMES

Agapornis fischeri 130
Alectoris graeca chukor 133
Amadina fasciata 67
Amandava amandava 55
Amauresthes fringilloides 86
Ara ararauna 131
Auripasser luteus 123 (124)

Bathilda ruficauda 106 (107)
Bombycilla cedrorum 120

Carduelis carduelis 74
Chloebia gouldiae 75
Chloropsis aurifrons 73
Coliuspasser macrourus 123
Coracias benghalensis 103
Cyanerpes caeruleus 109
Cyanerpes cyaneus 110
Cyanocorax affinis 82 (83)

Eodice malabrica cantans 104 (105)
Eophona personata 80
Erythrura prasina 96 (97)
Estrilda melpoda 118
Estrilda subflava 116
Estrilda troglodytes 116 (117)
Euplectes afra afra 121
Excalfactoria chinensis 101

Gallicolumba luzonica 136
Garrulax leucolophus 83
Geopelia c. cuneata 70
Gracula religiosa indica 132
Granatina granatinus 118 (119)
Gubernatrix Cristata 62

Hypargos niveoguttatus 114

Irene puella 72
Ixulus flavicollis 81

Lagonosticta caerulescens 84 (85)
Lagonosticta larvata vinacea 73
Leiothrix lutea 99
Leucopsar rothschildi 90
Lonchura castaneothorax 65
Lonchura domestica 56
Lonchura maja 87
Lonchura malabrica cantans 104, (105)
Lonchura malacca atricapilla 84 (86)
Lonchura punctulata 104 (106)
Lophortyx californicus 100
Lophura n. nycthemera 135
Loriculus galgulus 128

Mandingoa nitidula 112 (113)
Melopsittacus undulatus 58 (59)

Neophema bourkii 91
Neophema elegans 92
Neophema pulchella 95 (96)
Neophema splendida 95
Nymphicus hollandicus 66

Padda oryzivora 81 (82)
Paroaria cucullata 64
Paroaria dominicana 63
Parvo cristatus 134
Poephila acuticauda 76
Poephila cincta 98
Poephila gouldiae 75
Poephila guttata 125
Poephila personata 77 (78)
Psephotus haematonotus 93 (94)
Psittacula cyanocephala 93
Psittacula Krameri manillensis 133
Pycnonotus melanicterus 60
Pyrrhura frontalis frontalis 127

Quelea quelea 102

Ramphastos toco 136 (137)

Serinus canaria 61
Serinus mozambicus 78 (79)
Spreo superbus 108
Staganopleura guttata 68 (69)
Steganura paradisea 122
Stizoptera bicheonovii 57
Streptopelia senegalensis 70 (71)
Sturnus erythropygius andamanensis 88
Sturnus pagodarum 88 (89)

Tangara guttata 112
Thraupis cyanocephala 111
Tokus erythrorhynchus rufirostris 128
   (129)
Tauraco leucotis 138

Uraeginthus bengalus 115

Yuhina nigrimentum 124

Zosterops palpebrosa 126